Virtual S

Your privacy i. ... information society

The British Computer Society

BCS is the leading professional body for the IT industry. With members in over 100 countries, BCS is the professional and learned Society in the field of computers and information systems.

BCS is responsible for setting standards for the IT profession. It is also leading the change in public perception and appreciation of the economic and social importance of professionally managed IT projects and programmes. In this capacity, the Society advises, informs and persuades industry and government on successful IT implementation.

IT is affecting every part of our lives and that is why BCS is determined to promote IT as the profession of the 21st century.

Joining BCS

BCS qualifications, products and services are designed with your career plans in mind. We not only provide essential recognition through professional qualifications but also offer many other useful benefits to our members at every level.

BCS membership demonstrates your commitment to professional development. It helps to set you apart from other IT practitioners and provides industry recognition of your skills and experience. Employers and customers increasingly require proof of professional qualifications and competence. Professional membership confirms your competence and integrity and sets an independent standard that people can trust. Professional Membership (MBCS) is the pathway to Chartered IT Professional (CITP) status.
www.bcs.org/membership

Further Information

Further information about BCS can be obtained from: BCS, First Floor, Block D, North Star House, North Star Avenue, Swindon, SN2 1FA, UK.
Telephone: 0845 300 4417 (UK only) or + 44 (0)1793 417 424 (overseas)
www.bcs.org/contact

Virtual Shadows

Your privacy in the information society

Karen Lawrence Öqvist

 BCS

The British Computer Society
Publishing and Information Products
First Floor, Block D
North Star House
North Star Avenue
Swindon
SN2 1FA
UK

www.bcs.org

ISBN: 978-1-906124-09-0

British Cataloguing in Publication Data.
A CIP catalogue record for this book is available at the British Library.

Typeset by Sunrise Setting Ltd.
Printed in Great Britain by CPI Antony Rowe, Chippenham, Wiltshire

Contents

List of Figures and Tables

Author

Karen Lawrence Öqvist is a Security Solution Architect with Hewlett-Packard, residing in Sweden and working internationally. She started her career in IT 20 years ago in the UK. Her interest in digital identities was sparked at CERN, Geneva in 1996, which quickly grew to a passion that drove her to join Novell, the identity company, in 2000.

She has a Masters Degree in Information Security from the Royal Holloway University of London and has published several articles on identity and privacy. She is a frequent speaker at conferences both on the subject of identity and privacy, and information security management.

'Whenever a conflict arises between privacy and accountability, people demand the former for themselves and the latter for everyone else.'

DAVID BRIN, The Transparent Society, 1998

Acknowledgement

For my husband, Leslie, who believes in me.

List of Abbreviations

ADD	Attention Deficit Disorder
APEC	Asia-Pacific Economic Cooperation
ARCH	Action Rights for Children
ASD	Autism Spectrum Disorder
CALEA	*Communications Assistance for Law Enforcement Act*
CCTV	Closed-Circuit Television
DPA	*Data Protection Act*
ELSI	Ethical, Legal and Social Issues
ETSI	European Telecommunication Standardization Institute
GPS	Global Positioning System
IAD	Internet Addiction Disorder
ICAO	International Civil Aviation Organization
ICRA	Internet Content Resource Association
ILETS	*International Law Enforcement Telecommunications Seminar*
IM	Instant Messenger
IRC	Internet Relay Chat
ISA	Information Sharing and Assessment
ISP	Internet Service Provider
ISSA	Information Systems Security Association
ITU	International Telecommunications Union
LBS	Location-Based Services
LSC	Learning and Skills Council
MIAP	Managing Information Across Partners
MMORPG	Massively Multiplayer Online Role Playing Game
MMS	Multimedia Messaging Service
MoU	Memorandum of Understanding
MRTD	Machine-Readable Travel Document

NIR	National Identity Register
PICS	Platform for Internet Content Selection
PII	Personally Identifiable Information
PKU	Phenyle–Ketone–Uria
RFID	Radio-Frequency Identification
RIPA	*Regulation of Investigatory Powers Act 2000*
RSS	Really Simple Syndication
SMS	Short Message Service
VoIP	Voice over IP
WoW	World of Warcraft
WRITE	Web, Real-time, Interactivity, Technology, Expectations
YJB	Youth Justice Board
YOT	Youth Offending Team

Preface

I started to write this book while I was writing my master's thesis in Information Security at the Royal Holloway University of London in 2004. The title of my paper was 'Protecting Children as Active Users on the Internet'. From here I discovered a new online world, one that I was not really aware of, despite having 15 years of experience under my belt in IT. I discussed my findings with other IT colleagues who had children, to discover their perceptions of online communications and relationships. It was quite clear that, despite being IT experts and many of us gurus in our subject space, we had absolutely no idea. None of us had really stepped back to take a proper look at where these information highways that we had helped build over the last 20 years were taking us. What was really incredible is that it was our children who were taking this journey for us.

The paper that I finished in 2005 was focused on how the online world presented a threat to our children's safety: a virtual sandbox that was not safe for children. It was a virtual world designed by adults for adults that had been invaded by children from all over the world, all shapes, colours and languages, communicating and playing online. I started to write this book in the same context, but it never got finished because I discovered Web 2.0 and what it really meant. I set up my blog, got a Second Life, and created some online identities. Over time I built my online reputation.

This book embraces Web 2.0 as the future and asks whether Web 3.0 will bring us new surprises. The book continues the work of my thesis by questioning each of us about how we are sharing our personal information, not just online but also offline. There has been an endemic growth on the use of surveillance in our information society. Even us as parents contribute to this growth: we encourage the use of closed-circuit television (CCTV) in nurseries, so that we can observe our children over the internet; we track their movements via their mobile phone; we have their biometrics stored in a database at their schools; there are even initiatives gaining momentum to tag our children and link this in to the Global Positioning System (GPS). This is just the beginning. The subject space is vast and will have an impact on each and every one of us, whether we like it or not.

As such the privacy implications are profound. Information about us, which we may have shared or which has been collected, that we are aware of or not, could end up anywhere in the world and proliferate exponentially during our lifetime. That is the subject of this book: your virtual shadow, your privacy in a changing world and the implications for our children and our grandchildren in what we make to be tomorrow's world.

Karen Lawrence Öqvist

1 Introduction

The base assumption of the right to personal privacy has been recognised around the world in diverse regions and cultures. It is protected in the *Universal Declaration of Human Rights*, the *International Covenant on Civil and Political Rights* and in many other international and regional human rights treaties. Nearly every country in the world includes a right to privacy in its constitution, and if it is not defined explicitly, it is generally acknowledged implicitly as a right. However as quickly as privacy regulations are agreed between participating countries and codified as law, surveillance is growing on an endemic scale. There has been significant speculation as to whether we are 'sleepwalking into a surveillance age' as predicted by the UK Information Commissioner in 2004. The current situation could in fact be likened to the 'boiling frog' syndrome.

Leopold Stomm (1924–2003), the great political and economic theorist and amateur naturalist is said to have been the first to have observed that:

'If you drop a frog into a pan of boiling water it will leap out. However if you put a frog in a pan of cold water and gradually increase the heat until it is boiling, it will stay there until it is scalded to death. . . . sometimes we need to be aware of things that creep up on us before it is too late!'

To facilitate this trend, governments around the world have enacted legislation intended to comprehensively increase their reach into the private life of every living person. Hence, it does not matter where we live, what we do or who we are, this has an impact on every one of us. Action taken in the name of national security, encompassing law enforcement, the fight against terrorism, illegal immigration and welfare fraud, has effectively left the fundamental right to privacy fragile and exposed. The 'Information Age' has unleashed a surveillance society. This is not something in our future: it is the situation we face today. It has become so much a part of our everyday lives that it is difficult for even those ostriches amongst us to ignore. You know that there are those of us that find it convenient to bury our heads in the sand. It's nice there, cool, dark and it feels kind of safe.

Indeed wherever we go and whatever we do in our everyday lives, our personal information is being collected somewhere by someone or something. Sometimes we are aware of this, although more often we are not.

If this is not enough our willingness to share personal information has evolved: we have for years been sharing our personal and often sensitive data with government authorities and normally we do not have much choice in this. Even where we do have choice, we do it anyhow. We are easily enticed to take out loyalty cards (store cards, air-miles etc.) that give us privileged status with our favourite store, airline etc. This can actually feel nice and may give us a feeling of belonging, increased importance and status with the card provider. Many of us that possess these cards have no idea what has been done with our personal data. There are no automated mechanisms in place to inform us of how our personal information is being used.

What actually happens is that we are profiled. Profiling is achieved through advanced data-mining techniques. This takes the information collected on us and using special techniques we are effectively profiled or grouped by who we are and by what we do. Profiling is performed both in private industry and by public sector authorities. For example somebody with a criminal record would be profiled as such and probably profiled by the seriousness of their crime. It could be profiling by race, colour, gender or creed etc. Once created these profiles are attached to our identities and can influence decisions made about us over which we have no control. Profiling by organisations is normally used to retain customer loyalty, i.e. by tailoring your buying experience specifically to you or at least making it feel that way. The continued and growing use of profiling may result in a world whereby preferences and choices are made for us. This could make our lives more comfortable or on the other hand make our lives quite untenable if the outcome is some form of discrimination.

Then there is the subject of children, a generation that is growing up in a society that is surveyed, and a generation that is comfortable with the consequences of the information society. Most children have had mobile phones since their first day at school. They exploited the potential of Short Message Service (SMS) while adults were still using phones simply for their intended initial use, as speaking devices. Children love the built-in cameras and load these pictures onto their PC. These pictures end up on their blog, online and open to the world. This brings with it new risks, or perhaps the same risks with a new guise, in the protection of children.

Finally there is the recent explosion of computing power that has caused us to enter a new phase as we move towards a world of collaboration and social networks (Web 2.0) and ubiquitous computing. A paradigm shift has occurred; the rules of communication have changed raising a whole new connotation to the definition of 'information exposure' in the domain of information security when applied within the context of social networking. Individuals publish private information about themselves, their families and their friends on the web knowingly and willingly, although perhaps naive to the potential risks. Exposed information can be used for malicious purposes including the online-grooming of children, identity theft and the collection of private information for spamming.

Hence networking and collaboration are the buzzwords along with a growing awareness that, in addition to our physical life, we can also have multiple virtual identities (our digital shadow). Whether you are online as yourself or under a pseudonym you will inevitably over time build one or more online reputations linked to the associated virtual identity. Clearly as any individual may have many virtual identities, it is highly probable that a portion of these could present some linkage to their physical identity and consequently have an impact on their reputation in the real world. Any information that you or others share or post will quickly become 'digital information residue', i.e. personal information that has been collected or shared and digitally stored somewhere by someone or something in cyberspace. This brings to mind some questions concerning our identity, such as 'What is our identity?' and 'Are we at threat of losing control of whom we are or whom we are perceived to be today and tomorrow?'.

We start this book in Chapter 2 by examining how perceptions of our personal privacy are changing. We give the background as to why this is happening, which helps to put the subject matter for the rest of the book into context. In Chapters 3 and 4 we look at online safety, both for you and your children. Finally we close the book with Chapter 5 which provides an aerial view of the privacy landscape. We raise key concerns and attempt to structure them in ways that are simple to formulate and hence understand, in an information society where the rules of play have not yet been defined.

2 The Online Information Society

THE JOURNEY

The second renaissance?

The first information revolution occurred around 1448 following the invention of 'moveable type' for commercial use by Johannes Gutenberg (NationMaster.com 2008a). The idea was to cast individual letters (type) and then compose (move) these to make up printable pages. This threatened to disrupt the mainstream media of the day, performed by monks who painstakingly transcribed texts or carved entire pages into wood blocks for printing. Within decades moveable type spread across Europe, turbo-charging an information age known as the Renaissance. The age of mass media had arrived. Two more technological breakthroughs occurred in the 19th century that brought communication to new heights with the Cooke and Wheatstone telegraph patented in 1837 (About.com 2008a) followed almost 40 years later with the telephone in 1876. In fact 1876 not only marked the birth of Alexander Bell's telephone but also the death of the telegraph (About.com 2008b). Finally the media revolution reached its height in the 20th century with the invention of radio and television.

The second information revolution was ignited in 1990 by Sir Tim Berners-Lee who invented the World Wide Web (WWW) at CERN (the European Organisation for Nuclear Research, http://www.info.cern.ch) in 1989 along with the first web browser and editor and the first versions of the Hypertext Transfer Protocol (HTTP) and Hypertext Markup Language (HTML). Before then it was possible for computers to communicate over a network, but it was not very user friendly (Elon University 2008). In 1991 the first website appeared at http://info.cern.ch. In 1993 CERN announced that the web was to be free for anyone to use. Of course unbeknown to us there was a whole load of other stuff going

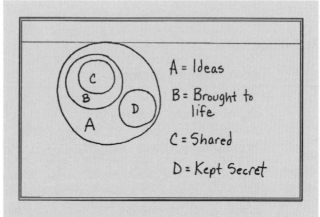

A = Ideas

B = Brought to life

C = Shared

D = Kept Secret

SHARING
'So you've got this idea.
It's a marvellous idea.
It'll change the world.
It's the answer to every prayer ever said.
It's beautiful.
It's simple.
It's perfect.
But you're stranded on a desert island.
With no Wifi.
Nobody to talk to.
A soggy Blackberry.
No bottles, no paper, and no pens.
So much for that idea.'

JESSICA HAGY, *The Age of Conversation*,
http://indexed.blogspot.com/

on behind the scenes before the birth of the web as we know it today. Hackers and IT gurus all over the world were frequenting newsgroups maintained by Compuserve and using Internet Relay Chat (IRC) as the principle chat medium.

In 1995 the internet had fewer than 20 million users. By 1999, when the number of users had reached 150 million, dotcoms were being formed, but when the technology bubble burst in 2001, thousands of firms were swept away. The survivors now operate in a market with over one billion users worldwide and this number is growing. Driving the strategy of these firms is the shifting behaviour of the consumers. eBay's business in particular has been moulded by its users. *Network effects* (a network effect creates value for a website based upon how many other people use the website) mean that the larger eBay becomes, the more addictive it becomes for both buyers and sellers. Much the same can be said for Google's role as the online advertising agency of choice, with firms paying for search links to ensure their products can be 'Googled'.

From the couch potato to the web potato

Baby boomers of the 1950s through to the 1970s grew up in a culture of TV dinners and passive listening. They were born to the notion of a guaranteed job for life. This was in a world where it was a normal expectation for their employer, social services and the government to take an active role in the responsibility for their wellbeing. On the contrary today in the 21st century we have been forced to take responsibility for our own lives. We have to create our own stability; hence we cannot expect any guarantee for a future that in anyway parallels the stability offered to parents and grandparents of the baby boomer generation. We are today living in a chaotic world in the midst of an information revolution, which is driving at a speed and ferocity that equals nothing that has ever been experienced before.

Email was how it started for most of us at the office. Somebody had the bright idea of installing an email server, thus bringing digital communication to the workplace. Digital communications have since spread from the workplace into the comfort of our homes. The computer that was once delegated to that 'third bedroom' or study has since migrated into the living area of many of our homes. The computer has hence become part of the family circle and has been promoted to the same status as the television. Broadband is becoming the norm for most families independent of where we live, as long as there is the infrastructure in place.

In addition few families today choose to live close together and with this the traditional extended family unit of the past is rapidly disappearing. Today's 60-year-old can no longer expect to be actively involved in the upbringing of their grandchildren and neither can they expect the younger generation to take on the role of carer once age and associated illnesses take their ugly toll. Today's aging population needs to adapt and learn to communicate in a different way in order to keep their active and rewarding role in the family circle, because how we communicate today has changed.

The early adopters of the information revolution were the first to jump on the bandwagon having understood that the parameters of how we communicate were shifting. In response, they were quick to migrate their snail-mail to email and replace local activities with involvement in online forums and communities where they could contribute to what mattered to them with people of similar motivations. Next they set up their blog, which provided the link to their physical friends, their virtual friends, their children and their grandchildren.

In fact by bringing the family unit together online, in a virtual sense of the word, early adopters have succeeded in cheating geography and physical factors that would usually prevent a normal family unit from being together. Hannah Greenham describes her own experiences as a mother of four children and someone whose own mother has proven to be an early adopter when it comes to getting an online presence.

'I am amazed by the relationship between my Mum and my children, compared to the relationship I had with my
(Continued)

(Continued)

grandmother and not just how we are changing, but the change it is forcing upon others. My Mum (who Steve praises highly as a silver surfer!) knows that to have good contact with her children, then she needs to be where her children are – and that means electronically too. I am proud that my 64 year old mother has a Face Book account. Steve delights that when we return from our holidays and he uploads the 400 or so digital photos that we've taken in two weeks, that within 24 hours, he either has an e-mail or the smugmug gallery has a scattering of comments; it's great that I can send her a URL of what the kids want for Xmas and she can e-choose before replying to my e-mail; I love it that we have webcams so the kids can come home from school and wave their creations of the day at a camera and she can delight in seeing them. Of course, nothing replaces the physical arms of a grandmother scooping a thrilled child up high into the air, but when we live two hours drive away, rather than two streets away (as I did), this is a fantastic relationship enhancer.'

The 'me' culture

Just as the UK 'baby boomers' learnt to think of 'me' during the 1980s, today's 'baby boomlets' or the 'Gen Y' (basically the grown-up babies of the 'baby boomers'; Time Magazine (2007)) have really got the 'me' culture moving. Born between 1980 and 2000, they have never known life without a computer. The 'Gen Y' is not waiting to 'earn' its luxury products: they feel entitled to them already. Their appetites have been 'wet-ted' by the doting baby boomer parents: they get what they want when they want it, either on their parents' credit cards or on their own.

Along with this is the unsaid expectation that their needs should be understood implicitly. They should not need to explain, it is the role of the rest of the world, also full of 'Gen Y', to meet their expectations. Hence we can anticipate the world of the future to be motivated by the need for comfort and luxury (alongside the growing efforts to reduce global warming). This provides a fertile ground for a diminishing 'need' for personal privacy and the eventual evolution to an environment that is able to respond to their needs based on what is learnt about each of them.

THE BLOGOSPHERE

> 'Web 2.0 celebrates individuality and it connects people because the art of creation is the act of being social.'
>
> JARON LANIER, Science Advisor at Linden Labs

Web 1.0 mirrored the physical world in a virtual space, whereas Web 2.0 is about people. Web 2.0 is a tool for bringing together the small contributions of millions of people in a user-powered revolution for democracy and human rights. Web 2.0 symbolises that a paradigm shift has occurred in how we are communicating and socialising, in a way that embraces collaboration and social networking, conveying a world where we willingly share our personal information online with the rest of the world and this is just the beginning!

Did you know that a blog is a website where entries are made in a journal style (postings) and displayed in a reverse chronological order. A posting can contain content resembling a personal diary or content on a specific subject space, e.g. cars, trains, your pets, family, etc. A blog can be about anything. Most blogs are primarily textual although some focus on photographs (photoblogs), videos (vlogs) or audio (podcasting). All blogs are part of a wider network of social interaction.

This phenomenon was brought to the attention of the public by *Time Magazine* that appointed 'The Person of the Year 2006 as You' (Time Magazine 2006), thus putting a face on the masses that have helped to shape the information age in a myriad of ways. The implication here is that each one of us has collectively made a contribution to the major milestones acknowledged as significant during 2006. For example it is the collaborative efforts of individuals that have made Wikipedia such a powerful tool; at amazon.com we review books and products online and collectively have the power to sway public opinion; we form virtual communities and use virtual spaces such as MySpace, Flickr and YouTube. It has become cool to have a blog, both professionally and socially, facilitating networking on a global scale. This is independent of geography, race, colour, creed, gender, age or disability; we are communicating and collaborating on a magnitude never seen before, bringing equality in a way never experienced before.

In March 2003, the *Oxford English Dictionary* added the terms blog (both noun and verb) and web log. Their definition of blog is that

'Blogs . . . contain daily musings about news, dating, marriage, divorce, children, politics in the Middle East . . . or millions of other things or nothing at all.'

The word 'blog' dates back to 1997 when one of the few practitioners at the time, Jorn Barger, called his site a 'weblog'. In 1999 another user, Peter Merholz, broke the word into 'we blog' and somehow the new term 'blog' stuck as both a verb and a noun (The Economist 2006a). In March 2003, the *Oxford English Dictionary* added the terms blog (both noun and verb) and web log and in 2004 Merriam-Webster, a publisher of dictionaries, had 'blog' as its word of the year. Technically a blog means a webpage to which its owner regularly adds new entries or 'posts' which tend to be (but need not be) short and often contain hyperlinks to other blogs or websites. In addition to text and hypertext posts can also contain pictures (known as 'photoblogs') and video (known as 'vlogs'). Each post is stored on its own distinct archive page called a 'permalink', where it may always be found. According to Technorati (a search engine for blogs) today a new blog is created every second of the day. There were 75 million blogs by early 2007 and there are 130,000 more created every day (Beck 2007). On average Technorati tracks some 50,000 new posts an hour. Technorati is integrated with the tools that power the blogosphere and is therefore notified of new content as it happens. Technorati lets you know what is being said right now, by whom and how it affects you. This means that if you make a posting on your blog Technorati will pick this up, which of course is very important if you want your visitors to keep returning.

Blogging is something we can all get involved with. In recent years blogging has evolved so that you no longer require any technical knowledge to blog: the tools are there, even for the technophobes among us. The blogosphere has become very accessible: we can upload pictures, video clips and songs with just a few clicks. Social networking spaces such as MySpace have made this very easy.

> 'Many ordinary people are scared of blogging because they feel that they have nothing to say. Yet mundane is interesting; it's OK to talk about your sandwich. To a handful of people in the world it may mean a lot.'
>
> MENA TROTT, President of Six Apart

Many of us have not blogged for a variety of reasons including a fear of lost privacy or the feeling that we have nothing interesting to say. However this is changing as products are coming onto the market that enable us to blog only to those to which we have something to say and also ensure our privacy. Mena Trott has developed one such tool herself: her company Six Apart is the product of this. She was blogging in the days when no such tools existed and wanted to keep the blog that she wrote for her family and close friends separate from the rest of the world. Nowadays in Facebook and MySpace you have 'friends and friends', i.e. those that you add to your friends list because you feel that it would be impolite and maybe politically incorrect not to do so (e.g. your boss) and those that are really your friends and family.

The main misconception about blogs is that they are only personal diaries. In fact weblogs come in all flavours, from personal journals that are mainly shared with close friends and family, to blogs with readership levels placing them in the league of mainstream media. Blog topics include political commentary, product reviews, scientific endeavours and any area of information where people have expertise and a desire to express it.

The power of blogs is that they allow millions of people to easily publish their ideas and millions more to comment on them. Blogs are a fluid, dynamic medium, more akin to a 'conversation' than to a library, which is how the web has often been described in the past. We like to show the world that we exist, what we do in our lives and what we think. We even publish photos and videos of ourselves online and it is becoming increasingly common for young people to meet and date online. We visit social networking sites, create profiles and share them with our friends, family and acquaintances. With an increasing number of people reading, writing and commenting on blogs, the way we use the web is shifting in a fundamental way. Instead of primarily being passive consumers of information, more and more internet users are becoming active participants. Weblogs allow everyone to have a voice.

Although online networking has been around via the use of usenets and newsgroups since the inception of the web, social networking as we know it today only really started to gain momentum around five to six years ago. MySpace,

Facebook and Friendster are among the most popular global sites and there are also sites adapted to regional needs and localised with languages.

It was back in 2003 that Friendster emerged as the first large-scale social networking site. Urban-dwelling 20 and 30 somethings were flocking to the site to model their social networks and meet new people. Friendster got a surprise because they expected that these users would use the site in a similar way to how they socialised in the physical world, i.e. only listing friends that they knew personally in their friends list. However this was not what early adopters did, they used Friendster to connect to other individuals that could be friends, those they partied with or friends of friends or just those with similar interests. In an attempt to keep the site intimate Friendster limited users from surfing to profiles beyond four degrees. This is because they were not receptive to Fakesters (collectors) when they first started appearing. Fakesters are those profiles that do not represent a real person. For example it could be a rock band or a cartoon character. The reaction of Friendster was to begin the deletion of all Fakesters when two particular Fakesters accumulated more than 10,000 friends each. The mass deletion of Fakesters was afterwards referred to as the Fakester genocide (Boyd and Heer 2006) and it gave MySpace what they needed in order to take the lead in the social networking space. Although Friendster has since changed its attitude, it was too late as the damage was already done.

Since its inception anything goes in MySpace. MySpace embraces the practice of fake profiles (collectors, Fakesters etc.). One of MySpace's early strategies was to provide a place for everyone who was rejected from Friendster. For example rock bands that had been deleted from Friendster were some of the earliest MySpace users. Over time movie stars, politicians, porn divas, comedians and other celebrities joined the party. It could be that the person behind the profile was not the celebrity but the manager. Moreover corporations began creating profiles for their products and brands. By taking this liberal approach MySpace always managed to hold a competitive advantage over Friendster even when Friendster eventually started to permit Fakesters.

Other social networking spaces include: Lunarstorm, Sweden's biggest social networking space; Mixi, which went public on the Tokyo Stock Exchange in September 2006 as the most popular blog space for young Japanese; CyWorld in South Korea; Bookie.com, one of China's biggest blogging sites; StudiVZ in Germany; and Hi in Peru.

At MySpace you can befriend anyone and anything; this is what makes MySpace so popular. A cat can have a profile as can a rock band. Any brand, political candidate or non-profit organisation can create a profile and start adding friends. You can click on your friends and see who they are friends with, click on their friends who happen to have the same interests as you and add them as one of your friends. MySpace is a mishmash of modern media: it is rich with music, video and comedy and is chaotic, loud and packed. Many user profiles are florid and flamboyant, with flashing text and pictures and music that starts playing as soon as you arrive. MySpace is an exciting place to be, but retaining your privacy on MySpace requires both vigilance and time. Most members do not even bother.

Another very popular social networking site is Facebook; founded at Harvard University in 2004, it quickly swept through college campuses. Facebook was only intended to be used to connect you to the people you already knew offline. It was a closed network and at the time you could not sign up without a college email address. Facebook began admitting highschool kids in 2005 and started hooking up with the workplace networks in April 2006 as graduates moved on into business. In 2008 it was touted as being the second most visited website in the United States. The look and feel of Facebook is uncluttered, clean and tidy. Unlike in MySpace the privacy mechanisms are built into the Facebook site as a default.

MySpace and Facebook may dominate the social networking space in the US market (Hitwise 2008a) but it is Bebo that has recently pulled ahead of MySpace in the UK. Facebook is the most visited website with Bebo at second place (Hitwise 2008b). Bebo has been around since 2005. The site resembles MySpace except it looks less cluttered. The site's privacy controls are some of the tightest online. Bebo is also available in Polish. Bebo alliances include a recent partnership with Yahoo! in September 2007 who sell the site's display ads in the UK and Ireland. Yahoo! will also integrate Yahoo! Answers with Bebo's site, so that users can ask and answer questions, and will develop a Bebo toolbar so that users can monitor their profiles whenever they are online. This follows a recently announced partnership with Microsoft that lets members Instant Messenger (IM) with anyone, Bebo friend or not, using Windows Live Messenger.

WHY BLOG?

WRITE

It does not matter who you are, what you do or how you look: as long as you can write and have an interest or passion in something, you are a potential blogger. But why blog, spending your free time online, communicating with what may feel a mostly unresponsive world when you could be doing something more useful?

Some bloggers started by using their blog as a personal diary and information contained online for the whole world to see can be perceived by many as quite personal. Some of these types of blogs could almost be likened to a form of therapy and linked with other blogs could in effect provide an environment similar to a peer support group. Gorski (2007) created an acronym to explain the writing/blogging/conversation phenomenon, WRITE.

Web: writing, through blogging, has created a 'world wide web' of connected people. Writing a blog might link you to new 'blog friends' and kindred spirits. As a group, you will share ideas, receive feedback and push creativity to higher levels.

Real-time: the response to writing happens almost immediately, ensuring that writing and ideas continue to flow. This immediately creates blogging benefits and challenges.

Interactivity: this creates the continually fresh online-classroom of learning.

Technology: this makes it all possible. Where will it take us next?

Expectations: keep them high, for yourself and others. Commit to writing you blog, the follow through. Comment on others' blogs, regularly. Connect. You will find gold.

Your blog as your personal diary or money-making machine

Heather Armstrong (online pseudonym Dooce; Figure 2.1) chronicles her life as a disenchanted Mormon in Salt Lake City, including her former career as a high-flying web designer in

FIGURE 2.1   *Blogger Heather Armstrong, alias Dooce*

Los Angeles and how she felt following her pregnancy and postpartum depression. She integrated pay-per-click advertising into her blog and about one to two years ago, her blog started to generate enough advertising revenue to become the main source of income for her family. She has about 1 million visitors to her blog every month that has taken five years to build. Evidence of this is seen on her blog. For example a posting she made on 19 September 2008, 'For now her name is Puppy', received 2,077 comments. You can visit her blog at http://www.dooce.com/.

Belle de Jour's blog ran on a similar vein and can be found at http://belledejour-uk.blogspot.com/. Belle de Jour is the pseudonym of a London prostitute that chronicled her life in her blog. The content of her blog was quite explicit and many that visited her blog were drawn back time after time, fascinated by what she wrote about her lifestyle. In 2003 the blog of Belle de Jour: diary of a London call girl was selected by *The Guardian* as blog of the year. Since the award the London prostitute has published several books.

> 'Archly transgressive, anonymous hooker is definitely manipulating the blog medium, word by word, sentence by sentence far more effectively than any of her competitors. It's not merely the titillating striptease aspects that are working for her, but her willingness to use this new form of vanity publishing to throw open a great big global window on activities previously considered unmentionable . . . She is in a league by herself as a blogger.'
>
> BRUCE STERLING, *The Guardian*

How your blog can make you famous

A blog could be likened to setting up a billboard and proclaiming to the world 'This is me! Listen to what I have to say about my little world'. Shi Hengxia (online pseudonym Hibiscus Sister) hosts a successful blog that receives the most traffic in China, so much so that she has started to appear on magazine covers and TV. Many Chinese say that they find her exhibitionist nature quite distasteful, clashing with the respectful nature of the Chinese culture. However despite this by the summer of 2005 she had become a nationwide celebrity. In August 2005 a number of blog sites were ordered to move Hibiscus Sister's postings to less trafficked areas, enabling her to complain that she was the victim of a 'crackdown' (Chandler 2006).

A blog that chronicles our lives, our opinions and those personal facts that we would traditionally have kept private has a cost. This cost is difficult to quantify: the loss of privacy is one cost, as is the risk that your online presence may in the future have an impact on your reputation in the real world, e.g. when life values change, as is prone to happen as we mature and get older. 'Washing your dirty laundry in public' is in today's society generally frowned upon. However this may change in the future as social attitudes adapt to this evolving online culture of communication and openness.

Start a blog to keep in touch

Some of us blog to keep in touch with our friends and families, and this is what Salam Pax did, a pseudonymous blogger from Iraq (Figure 2.2). Salam's site is titled after his friend Raed Jarrar, who was working on his master's degree in Jordan and was not in the habit of responding promptly to email. To keep in touch Salam set up the weblog for him to read. His site is called 'Where is Raed?'. Salam's site received notable media attention during (and after) the 2003 invasion of Iraq. His pseudonym is formed from the words for 'peace' in Arabic (Salām) and Latin (Pāx). In his blog, Salam discusses the war, his friends, the disappearances of people under the government of Saddam Hussein and his work as a translator for journalist Peter Maass. In May 2003 *The Guardian* newspaper tracked the man down and printed a story indicating that he did indeed live in Iraq, with the given name Salam and was a 29-year-old architect. Salam is an excellent writer: presenting amusing, honest and enjoyable reading on a subject that is extremely sensitive.

FIGURE 2.2   *Salam Pax,*
the 'Baghdad Blogger'
(reproduced by permission
of Chris Usher Photography
& Associates)

Meet the founding father of blogging

Where did it all start, this blogging? Well one of the earliest recognised bloggers is Justin Hall who began 11 years of personal blogging in 1994 while he was a student at Swarthmore College. He started his web-based diary 'Justin's Links from the Underground', which offered one of the earliest guided tours of the web. Over time his personal blog focused increasingly on his own life in intimate detail and over 11 years he composed more than 4,800 pages (SFGate 2005). Justin is an American freelance journalist. In December 2004 *New York Times Magazine* referred to him as 'the founding father of personal blogging'. This seems to indicate that in Justin's case being a blogger has in fact built his online reputation and it seems to have benefited his career as a journalist. Suddenly in 2005 Justin surprised everyone when he stopped blogging. It happened in mid-January when he made a short film called 'Dark Night' that he released on the internet. He replaced his ever-changing home page with a fixed red heart filled with question marks and his website moved from the present to the past tense. He left a search bar next to the questioning hearts, letting readers sift through the archives. However fortunately for all bloggers since 2005 he does still have an online presence: you can find his blog at http://www.links. net/ with some links that give information on what he is doing today.

Blogging to have a conversation

The blogosphere has seen several books published by bloggers. One worth a special mention is *The Age of Conversation* as the first book ever authored by 103 different bloggers, authors who have never met, from 10 different nations around the world. Published in July 2007, this unique 'blook' is a publishing phenomenon.

The challenge was to create a book with one theme and 100 authors. Each author contributed a chapter on a conversation, waived their rights for royalties and donated the profits from book sales to Variety, a children's charity. By December 2007 their collaborative efforts raised over US$11,000 for Variety. The success of *The Age of Conversation* has inspired the blogging community to team up to bring out a second edition in 2008 with even more authors and diverse themes.

Arun Rajagopal from Oman (in the Middle East) was one of the co-authors of *The Age of Conversation* (Figure 2.3). Following Arun's contribution to the book he made it into the Middle East media. In his efforts to promote the book he sent out a call to all Hewlett Packard (HP) bloggers, the present author included, naming them individually in his blog (http://www.arunrajagopal.com) and asking them to buy the book. He focused on HP bloggers as his chapter dealt with HP's erstwhile 'Rules of the Garage' management philosophy. Those HP bloggers who regularly 'Google' themselves found his call, his blog and the reference to the book.

Incidentally the book is well worth a read in that it encapsulates so beautifully how bloggers feel about blogging and why they blog and it can be found online at http://www.ageofconversation.com. *The Age of Conversation* is inspiring, every page individual in its content and each gives unique perspectives on social media. It is a must read for every blogger

FIGURE 2.3   *Arun Rajagopal, the famous
Middle East blogger*

and those inspired to step into this online world and join
the conversation.

CLIP CULTURE AND VLOGGERS

The blogosphere is full of talented 'wannabes' and there is no
better place to find them than on YouTube. People playing a
musical instrument, singing or playing a tune on a comb, talking dogs and dancing cats and more can all be found, and anyone can upload content to the site. The 'clip culture' is upon us.

Chad Hurley and Steve Chen created YouTube following a
dinner party where the guests who had camcorders complained how difficult it was to share videos.

Did you know that by the time of YouTube's official launch in December 2005, more than a million short video clips were already uploaded? On an average day 8,000 video clips were uploaded and 3 million were viewed.

Examples of successes include Andy McKee who is an American acoustic guitarist who became an online sensation after videos of his performances were posted on YouTube by his record label. In late 2007 a live performance of his flagship song 'Drifting' became a Featured Video on YouTube, achieving over 10 million views and earning a steady place as one of the highest rated music clips on the site.

Many people initially believed that Bree was a real internet vlogger creating a chronicle of her life as video that was subsequently posted to YouTube. However she was in fact an actress playing a role in an independent film project (*The Children of Anchor Cove*). This chronicle was not real, it was the life of a fictitious person. The discovery that Bree was actually actress Jessica Lee Rose received quite some media coverage in September 2006.

THE ONLINE SOCIETY AND NEW OPPORTUNITIES

'The word "wiki" comes from the Hawaiian word for "quick", but also stands for "what I know is . . .". Wikis are the purest form of participatory creativity and intellectual sharing, and represent "a socialisation of expertise".'

DAVID WEINBURGER, 2006

The information society is bringing us collaboration on a scale and in ways never seen before. The development of open-source software is one clear winner. Open-source software is software that does not belong to an organisation and is developed by a group of volunteers that normally communicate via the use of forums. These are often in the form of 'wikis'. Wikis are spaces that are often attributed to projects or spaces with a common theme. Those developers that contribute the most become well known in their own and other associated communities and over time this builds their online reputation.

Wikis can be found everywhere online in public spaces and in the workplace. Wikis can be described as webpages that allow anyone who is authorised to provide content. The most famous wiki worldwide is Wikipedia, where volunteers around the world are contributors. Wikipedia's promise on the liberation of human knowledge has been fulfilled. This has been achieved by enabling access to all spheres of society regardless of class or background. Wikipedia today is estimated to be at least 12 times larger than *Encyclopaedia Britannica* and is published in more languages: 200 at the time of writing of this book. Wikipedia has over 10 million articles, 25 per cent of them in English. Anyone can become a contributor and thousands of people all over the world have contributed. Amongst these contributors you find the hardcore contributors of a few hundred volunteers, who have dedicated all of their spare time to the fulfilment of this work. These are people who know each other (in the virtual sense of the word) and value their online reputations.

RELATIONSHIPS AT THE SPEED OF INFORMATION

Relationships are what we make of them. In this section we hear of the experiences of people that have used ecommunication, which has had a positive or negative impact on how they communicate or on their perceptions of communication. The first contribution is by Moira Sawbridge, known affectionately by her son-in-law as the 'Silver Surfer' because she is over 60 years old and internet savvy. Next Hannah Greenham tells us how she met her husband Steve online. Then we hear from the virtual mum who opens our eyes to the disparate family; and finally we discuss virtual cheating where we talk about two avatars that have married in Second Life and the consequences on their real lives. From this example a message can be understood. Do not underestimate the power of virtual relationships: they can make you or break you, just as physical relationships can in the real world. After all behind every email account, pseudonym and online computer is a real person sitting there waiting to have a conversation with you.

The silver surfer

'There are not many families today that are able to live close together, and with this the traditional family unit from the past is rapidly disappearing. Today's 60 year old can no longer expect to be actively involved in the upbringing of their grandchildren nor can they expect the younger generation to take the role as carers once age and associated illnesses take their ugly toll.

As with all great things, they come to an end eventually, and this day has arrived for the beloved snail-mail; with first the phone and then the internet.

Now long or short notes can be sent quickly, read at the receiver's convenience, and if appropriate, a reply sent straight away. So little 'unimportant' messages, which would never be justified in writing down put in an envelope, stamped, and taken to the post can now be communicated and sometimes replied to before you would even have got out of the house to go to the post box! In so doing it 'feels' as if the person is present with you having a conversation, or at least only as far away as the garden fence.

Phoning is not the equivalent alternative to e-mailing. It is not always convenient to answer the phone let alone have a chat however much you want to. The person making the call is the one who it suits and yet they could still be in a rush, and even with pre-arranged calls you can not be sure it is still convenient for the person at the other end to devote that time to speaking to you. E-mailing fits in with everyone's timetable. No need to check time changes around the world, work shift patterns or the school

(Continued)

(Continued)

run etc. So being in contact can be constant as sending on information from the internet is easy and fast and you can forward it along with photos etc. All this enhances e-mail relationships because of the EASE and SPEED. No cutting out newspaper cuttings, getting extra photos printed, copying down addresses etc to send by post or leave by the phone to convey verbally at a later time. What is more if you want to read the communication on paper it can still be printed at the other end!'

MOIRA SAWBRIDGE, November 2007

Virtual equality and Mr Right

'I knew I would marry my husband Steve before I'd even met him.

I first got to e-know him through an on line conferencing system, Cix, back in 1995. He was there in a professional capacity—a self confessed computer geek, hanging out with other computer geeks! I was there because I had an impatient boss who wanted an e-mail address before the managers of the department we were working in were ready to furnish everyone with this new technology!

With the help of a friend at work, who worked in our computer department, I bought my first second hand PC and modem. Online I realised that I could be who I wanted to be. I created an identity—with a mock name and mock picture! I created a resume, noting the good things in my life and not the bad. The whole experience was quite liberating.

In those days I shared a house with another "Cixen" as Cix users were affectionately known. He ran and moder-ated a conference called "splitting up", where likeminded people could talk about just that—splitting up and all the mess it made! I had just come through a broken marriage myself. It was a closed conference, for members only, not

(Continued)

(Continued)

for the world to see. Talking about life with a small group of people was OK—that's like group therapy or counselling, isn't it?

Steve was one of the many chatty individuals in the conference, sharing the ups and downs of a relationship break up. Recently separated, with a child in tow, he sympathized with some of my laments and gave useful advice to others. One October evening, a pizza evening for "singles, lonely and desperates" was arranged. It wasn't really my thing but I tagged along anyway, as my housemate was right— I wasn't doing anything else and all the people that I normally chatted with online wouldn't be there tonight as, they would be out meeting each other and eating pizza.

When I arrived I was shocked by what a weird bunch of individuals I'd been spending my virtual time with! The thing that internet relationships don't have is prejudice. It doesn't matter if you have quirks or oddities, a strange job, lifestyle, tattoos, body piercing—e-relationships make us all the same; an ID at a cursor prompt.

So here I was in a room with the group of individuals that were really not "my type": a part time viking, a giant haystack style biker, a lady who would only eat poppadums, who was dating a vegan skinhead 30 years her junior and covered with body piercing, not forgetting the deaf computer programmer. I really felt out of my comfort zone. Whilst spending the evening with these people I learnt something about myself, and that was that I was prejudiced, and always had been. I realised that when I had walked into the room earlier, I had been so shocked by the initial appearance of these people that I had forgotten the months of e-friendship and support that they had given me.

I didn't see Steve that evening; in fact it was over 6 months later that Steve and I got back into contact again, although this time when we chatted it felt as though something had happened, our friendly banter had moved onto a different level. I felt more comfortable speaking to someone I knew already, and our chats weren't just about

(Continued)

(Continued)

our hobbies or coping with life post divorce, we were chatting in a way that two people who had known each other all their lives would. The more we talked, the more comfortable we were and the more we shared. We'd shared pictures of each other and although I'd never heard his voice and he'd never heard mine, it was bizarre that online we had succeeded in becoming soul mates. We had by then been chatting for many months on line and shared what felt like everything, hopes, dreams, anxieties and failings. We had become the modern day equivalent of pen pals, but working at e-speed meant the relationship went from acquaintance to intimate in months rather than years.

We agreed that it was time to meet in person; three days later we moved in together, life apart just did not seem to make sense. We have since married and raised four beautiful children!'

HANNAH GREENHAM, November 2007

The virtual mum

'Carrie Hammond watches as her 6-year old son, Kegan, tears through a slew of birthday gifts and cards, his excitement mounting with each one. She waits patiently for him to open the special present she has given him – a Magnetix Magnetic Building Set, dozens of colourful rods, spheres and cones held together by magnets to form endless shapes. The look on his face tells Hammond she made the right choice.

"Thank you, mum," he says, holding up the brightly colored box, almost forgetting about the accompanying birthday card. Later, although bedtime is approaching, Hammond gives in to Kegan's please for just one more game of tic-tac-toe, which he wins.

It's like any other birthday scene where a parent watches a child rifle through presents, with one exception: Hammond

(Continued)

(Continued)

is in California, and Kegan is in Tennessee. Their entire communication took place via the Internet.

Since Hammond and her husband divorced and she moved out of the state almost four years ago, this has been a twice-a-week ritual for mother and son. With inexpensive Webcams and microphones to help them share books, play games and catch up, virtual visitations have bridged the physical distance between them and made the separation a little more bearable.'

Delta Sky Magazine, 2006,
from an article on Virtual Visitation[1]

Virtual cheating

In the past 'cheating' on your partner normally referred to a physical relationship. However online this can be a virtual relationship in that there may not be any physical contact. There are cases in Second Life for example whereby partners have hired a virtual private detective to track their loved one in the virtual world to see if they are cheating virtually and ultimately having virtual sex.

'On a scorching July afternoon, as the temperature creeps toward 118 degrees in a quiet suburb east of Phoenix, Ric Hoogestraat sits at his computer with the blinds drawn, smoking a cigarette. While his wife, Sue, watches television in the living room, Mr. Hoogestraat chats online with what appears on the screen to be a tall, slim redhead.

He's never met the woman outside of the computer world of Second Life, he's never so much as spoken to her on the telephone. But their relationship has taken on curiously real dimensions. They own two dogs, pay a mortgage together and spend hours shopping at the mall and taking long motorcycle rides. [. . . . .] This May, when Mr. Hoogestraat, 53, needed real-life surgery, the redhead
(Continued)

(Continued)

cheered him up with a private island that cost her $120,000 in the virtual world's currency, or about $480 in real-world dollars. Their bond is so strong that three months ago, Mr. Hoogestraat asked Janet Spielman, the 38-year-old Canadian woman who controls the redhead, to become his virtual wife.

The woman he's legally wed to is not amused. "It's really devastating," says Sue Hoogestraat, 58, an export agent for a shipping company, who has been married to Mr. Hoogestraat for seven months. "You try to talk to someone or bring them a drink, and they'll be having sex with a cartoon."

[. . . . . .]

"There's a huge trust between us," says Ms. Spielman, a divorced mother of two who works in office sales in Calgary, Alberta, and began logging on to Second Life in January. "We'll tell each other everything."

That intimacy hasn't spilled into real life. They never speak and have no plans to meet. Aside from the details they share over Second Life instant messages, each knows little about the other beyond what's posted on their brief online user profiles.'

The Wall Street Journal Online, 2007

NEW AGE ADDICTIONS

Internet addiction has been acknowledged as a growing problem and is better known today as a more pure form of data addiction. This can come in the form of increasing how often your computer is checking for new emails to the flow of really simple syndication (RSS) feeds to your mobile phone. A growing addiction is having email come directly to your phone or your Blackberry (a device designed especially to give you 24/7 access to your email wherever you are).

There is much hype on the impact this is having on our physical lives and the associated dislocation from our immediate surroundings, as our dependence on a continuous flow of electronic information invades our very existence. We could claim it props up our egos and above all gives us a rising inability to be alone with our own thoughts. However another way of seeing this is as a different way of living: a different way of living with new problems, but often these are the same old problems with a new set of clothes. Some of these are covered in this section.

Information addiction

Two Harvard faculty members stated that information causes a 'dopamine squirt' in humans, a rush similar to that given by narcotics. Just as narcotics are addictive, information is as well. They have given the disorder of information addiction the name 'pseudo-ADD' (Impact Lab 2003) because it tends to cause attention deficit disorder (ADD)-like symptoms.

The ubiquity of technology in the lives of executives, other business people and consumers has created a subculture of the always on. For all of the efficiency gains that it seemingly provides, the constant stream of data can interrupt not just dinner and family time, but also meetings and creative time and it can prove very tough to turn off. Although the constant flow of information right into our hands gives us that instant 'information kick' and the feeling of self-importance, the longer-term impact of spending less time with others physically is more concrete and sustaining. Information addiction is a lifestyle choice. It is up to us to decide how we prioritise.

Internet addiction disorder

According to the Center for Internet Addiction,

> 'Internet addicts suffer from emotional problems such as depression and anxiety-related disorders and often use the fantasy world of the internet to psychologically escape unpleasant feelings or stressful situations.'

It is possible that a person could have a pathological relationship with a specific aspect of the internet, such as bidding on online auctions, viewing pornography or online gambling, but that does not make the internet medium itself addictive. So-called internet addicts do not suffer from the same level of damage to health and relationships that are common to established addictions. The availability of the internet just makes an addiction to one of these aspects more likely. The following list includes common addiction problems which the Center for Internet Addiction Recovery (http://www. netaddiction.com) states can be mistakenly classified as internet addiction disorder (IAD).

- A pathological gambler is a pathological gambler regardless of whether the gambling is done on a computer or face-to-face.
- A person with poor impulse control can lose sleep over a suspenseful novel or favourite television show just as easily as they can lose sleep over an exciting computer game or the temptation to click on another web link.
- A person with a sexual obsession is still a person with a sexual obsession, whether the pornography is viewed on a screen or on paper.
- A person who shops obsessively (including during a manic phase) has an obsessive shopping problem whether the purchases are made in person, by mail, by phone or online.
- A problem day trader, who has a form of pathological gambling, is still a problem day trader regardless of whether the stock trading is done by computer, over the phone or face-to-face.

Game addiction is also a growing problem among children and adults alike.

POWER TO THE PEOPLE

The citiyen

The globalisation of communication has brought a latent strength in numbers to the surface as people from all nations around the world rise up and speak out online. No longer are we, those of us whom happen live in the industrialised west, at the mercy of administrative bureaucrats, politicians and popular media, that in the physical world always seem to be able to have the last word. Web 2.0 allows us all to have a voice.

What is a citizen? After all a citizen is not only the state's customers but they are also its owners. The term often used in the jargon of government technology is '*citiyen*', reflecting the French idea of the politically engaged citizen. Technology can amplify and aggregate voices that used to be faint and muffled. Voters used to write letters to politicians and newspaper editors in the hope they would be listened to or published. Now they can blog. In December 2007 Technorati (http://www.technorati.com) was tracking more than 112 million blogs in the blogosphere.

In countries that live under suppressive regimes, the battle to control the internet and the impact it is having on their citizens in maintaining control of their perceptions of the world is proving quite difficult. China has had Google maintain special filters on the search engine to control what Chinese citizens can find. North Korea has effectively created a national 'intranet'. This intranet can be likened to a walled garden; North Korean online citizens cannot get out and those online from outside cannot get in. Pakistan caused chaos outside of its own country due to routing miscalculations and errors on the worldwide network by attempting to block 'blasphemous' videos in March 2008. It seems that Pakistan's attempts to block YouTube from their own population disrupted YouTube access around the world. This problem was gradually repaired although as a sidenote this does highlight some serious infrastructural issues on the internet.

This section takes some examples from around the world that give us 'food for thought' on how the dynamics of the world are changing. We each have a voice irrespective of gender, geography, creed, education etc. and in the information society these voices can influence policy makers in our world, and help them to make decisions that favour the majority as opposed to the minority. Whether this is for good or bad is for most of us a subjective judgement and depends on which side of the fence we happen to be sitting.

> 'Today people no longer passively consume media but actively participate in them, which usually means creating content, in whatever form. It could be as simple as rating the restaurant they went to or the movie they saw, or as sophisticated as shooting a home video.'
>
> ERIC SCHMIDT, Google

Wear something red on Friday

On Friday the 28 September 2007 there was a grand turnout of people around the world that turned up to work wearing the colour red in support of the monks and democracy in Burma. The full-blown synchronous support of so many on this day was triggered for a great number by an SMS they received the day before asking them to demonstrate their support by wearing red on Friday. It was a form of phone SPAM where all of those that had received this SMS were asked to send it on to a number of their friends. The result was that nearly every person in every main city in the world knew that on Friday they should wear red.

The Great Firewall of China

Since late 2005 Western media have been filled with reports of Beijing's increasingly heavy-handed attempts to silence dissent and block references to politically sensitive topics such as democracy and human rights. The debate is especially hot in the United States because some of America's most respected technical pioneers, many who tout the web as a force for individual empowerment, have collaborated with the Communist Party's efforts to keep the internet under control. Cisco and Sun Microsystems sell Beijing hardware and filtering systems used to block access to forbidden sites, the so-called Great Firewall of China managed by nine state-licensed internet-access providers that use technology and an army of censors to patrol the gateway between China and the rest of the world. In addition Google has deployed a separate, politically correct site for users in China which blocks access to content that Beijing considers controversial, the result being that when Chinese users 'Google' Tiananmen Square they get a list of pictures of tourists strolling around Mao's tomb, while the rest of the world are directed to links depicting the massacre that caused such global outrage.

A survey conducted by OpenNet Initiative a couple of years ago deemed China's filtering regime 'the most sophisticated effort in the world'. The list of what is forbidden is long and constantly updated. The problem is that the rules needed to maintain this list are long and complex, and hence impossible to enforce consistently, so some censored material does get through. China is said to have an army of censors called 'net nannies' thought to number in the tens of thousands that monitor computers in every home and over 100,000 internet cafés in China.

However the very nature of the web is creating a society that connects and communicates, bringing people together in the form of forums, blogs and wikis, hence celebrating the very democratic ethos of the right for individual choice. The internet is tipping the scales in favour of openness, as is the web as it brings people together from outside of the influence of the state. Before the online world became popular in China, the liveliest exchanges were found on bulletin boards and in chatrooms run by major portals. However these spaces were moderated by editors who casually removed any controversial postings. Things have changed. Today China has more internet users than any country in the world except for the United States and in 2006 they had over 16 million bloggers (Chandler 2006).

Blogs are more difficult to control than bulletin boards and forums because they are so easy to set up and can simply be moved between servers. The blogosphere within the Great Firewall of China is thriving and spreading word about a whole host of embarrassing incidents that were censored in

China's mainstream press, including a toxic chemical spill and a police crackdown on protestors that left 20 farmers dead (Chandler 2006). In addition Chinese users are becoming increasingly streetwise with a growing army of 'hacktivists' outside China working to help them slip past the blocks. A software program called Freegate allows Chinese users to circumvent the filters by connecting them to US servers. A network called Tor (The Onion Router; to find more information on how this works refer to the podcast by Steve Gibson by searching for 'Tor' at http://www.grc.com/SecurityNow. htm), based in Boston, enables Chinese users to send messages anonymously. The Great Firewall of China is starting to crumble. Thus the internet, even within its censored form, has become an enabler for free expression much to the vexation of Chinese Communist authorities. Today Chinese citizens enjoy greater freedom of thought and access to information from outside China than at any other time in history.

No ban for Facebook in the Middle East

'The internet has changed Saudi Arabia beyond anybody's wildest expectations. The virtual world of the internet provided my generation with a perspective on the world that the old generation lacks, especially for women.'

RAJAA ALSANEA *Time Magazine*, Spring 2008 Supplement

There were widespread rumours circulating in the United Arab Emirates (UAE) in early 2008 that the social networking site Facebook had been blocked after thousands of residents found themselves unable to access the site.

In fact the rumour was false; apparently there had been an outage that was due to 'technical/connectivity issues'. However the rumours that Facebook had been blocked were fuelled by previously implemented bans on other popular social networking sites, such as Orkut in July 2007 following reports that the site contained sexually explicit material and was being used for 'immoral activities', and Flickr and Hi5. MySpace and YouTube were also banned, but this has since been lifted. The only place in the UAE where the bans are not enforced is for those users based in free zone locations such as Dubai Internet City.

It looks as though social networking sites are in the UAE to stay. Maktoob.com and faye3.com have recently teamed up to develop their own Arab social networking site to rival Facebook. The two sites are working on a joint initiative aimed at providing a service that will allow Arab communities to link up online and share contacts.

Digital communications in the UAE are having some impacts on the female population. Novelist Rajaa Alsanea has published a book called *Girls of Riyadh* which is a tale of four young Saudi women and their romantic intrigues organised as a year-long series of juicy, tell-all emails that are sent out on Fridays (after prayers). The four women in this book used SMS to communicate. Along with these four main characters, the heroes of the novel are the internet and mobile phones. Initially the book was banned in Saudi Arabia, but the Saudi government intervened to allow distribution. The Saudi culture minister believes that such controversial books should be permitted in society to allow for healthy dialogue between the younger generations. Despite this the hate mail posted to the website created for readers' reactions hits 500–1,000 a day (Raper Larenaudie 2008).

The digital divide

'Social networking communities have allowed Africans to broadcast their individual experiences worldwide and engage their foreign counterparts in conversations about solving Africa's societal issues. Tools such as blogs, Skype and SMS are connecting people and accelerating the time it takes to exchange ideas and collaborate with Africans, hence changing the way development programs are organised.'

G KOFI ANNAN, Annansi.com/blog

What the 'digital divide' means to you depends on where you come from. In the industrialised world you often hear this phrase coined when referring to those people that do not have access to a computer and are consequently unable to go online. This means that they miss out on reduced costs for flights, car hire and holiday packages that are available by booking online and the convenience of other services, such as online government and banking services, which can feel like a form of discrimination for them.

In third world and developing countries, the digital divide refers to all people that do not have access to a digital infrastructure that enables them to go online and partake in a global community. This is particularly pertinent to children.

In 2002 MIT Professor Nicholas Negroponte experienced first-hand how connected laptops transformed the lives of children and their families in a remote Cambodian village. A seed was planted: If every child in the world had access to a computer, what potential could be unlocked? What problems could be solved? These questions eventually led to the foundation of One Laptop per Child (OLPC, http://laptop.org) and the creation of the XO laptop. The goal was to build a child-size computer that could withstand extreme conditions, such as heat, dust and extreme movement, and could run on solar-power (if there was no electricity).

The concept was that if a machine is designed smartly enough, without the bloat of standard laptops, and sold in large enough quantities, the price could be reduced dramatically to a point where developing countries could afford millions of them: one per child. The laptop is called the XO because if you turn the logo 90° it looks like a child. Applications native to the XO laptop are called activities and are available for download at an activity wiki. What is even more exciting is the social networking that is built into the XO: social sharing, mesh networks (connecting to their friends in the area) and WiFi (when internet is available). It can run on solar power and is built to withstand extreme conditions. The XO has no harddisk or CD-ROM. The initiative succeeded all expectations, except in the price. The marketable price was nearly US$200. In Canada they had a marketing initiative whereby if you bought one of these computers, one would also be sent to a child in Africa. With more initiatives like this let us hope that the digital divide for future generations living in third world and developing countries will disappear, so that they can be a part of the global online community and add to the voice of the people and feel that they make a difference in the world.

Asperger's Syndrome is no syndrome in a virtual world

There are an increasing number of Second Life residents that are there for serious reasons. They are part of support groups for cancer survivors. They build Buddhist retreats and meditate. Then there is the Brigadoon community. This community is a private haven where people dealing with Asperger's Syndrome or autism can practice their socialisation skills in an environment where everyone knows everyone else.

> 'People with autism are using the web in a totally different way. They have a social drive, but the exchange does not go through non-verbal stuff or emotional sharing, what they are interested in is sharing information. It bypasses all the non-verbal stuff, which they are not interested in.'
>
> LAURENT MOTTRON, an autism researcher and doctor at the University of Montreal in Canada

For example Torley Wong who is a project manager at Linden Labs in San Francisco, which created Second Life, is not the only person with an autism spectrum disorder (ASD) who prefers online communication to meeting people in the flesh. In the past few years, people with all forms of ASD, from Asperger's to the more severe forms known as 'low-functioning' or 'classic' autism, have taken to the Web, joining virtual worlds, writing blogs and posting videos on websites such as YouTube (New Scientist 2007).

> 'I can observe gestures, and watch them repeatedly, to learn body language, . . . It seems very odd off-line to tell someone to keep smiling for me, I want to pick up on that.'
>
> TORLEY WONG, Project Manager at Linden Labs

Torley uses interactions inside the virtual world to learn more about how to socialise off-line. He buys 'gestures', animations of avatars making faces, and plays them back to himself.

Many blogs and websites created by people with autism promote the idea of 'neural diversity', the notion that the condition is not a disease that must be cured, but simply a different brain 'wiring'.

It does not stop here, the concept of Second Life can be used for experimentation: a Petri dish for innovations that may help people in real life. Learning organisations today are using Second Life as a medium for long-distance learning and Crisis response groups for the rehearsal of responses to earthquakes and terrorist attacks.

> 'Peter Yellowlees, a professor of psychiatry at the University of California, Davis, has been teaching about schizophrenia for 20 years, but says that he was never really able to explain to his students just how their patients suffer. So he went online, downloaded some free software and entered Second Life. Peter created hallucinations. A resident might walk through a virtual hospital ward, and a picture on the wall would suddenly flash the word "shitface". The floor might fall away, leaving the person to walk on stepping stones above the clouds. A reflection in a mirror might have bleeding eyes.'
>
> *The Economist*, 28 September 2006

Imagine if we were to use the concept of virtual worlds more as a learning aid or experimental tool, to have the ability to get out of ourselves and see the world through the eyes of somebody else. Imagine if children were to learn history and geography by interacting with a virtual world in addition to learning the dates and facts from a textbook. Would this not help us to become better people who are less judgemental and open to new ideas?

The virtual hammer

eBay is the world's largest auction site. In November 2005 Google launched 'Google Base', a free service that allows users to upload anything including classifieds free-of-charge. The success of eBay is dependent upon the number of buyers and sellers that are using the service, referred to as 'network effects'. The more buyers and sellers there are, the more the service will grow.

Almost anything can be found on eBay with millions of items for sale worldwide, grouped into more than 40,000 main and sub-categories (*The Economist*, 11 June 2005). Both buyers and sellers have to be registered to trade, but anyone can look. Buyers can put in the most they are prepared to pay for an item and then eBay automatically bids on their behalf according to pre-determined increments; alternatively the shopper can buy immediately if sellers pay an insertion fee and then a final-value fee on goods that are sold. It is then up to the buyer and seller to contact each other to arrange payment and delivery.

eBay's simple online system relies to a certain extent on the fact that most people are basically honest. However as the market has grown so has the level of dishonesty. Category managers and eBay's security experts police the listings and provide advice to avoid scams and phoney items. Buyers and sellers who break the rules can be expelled. eBay's feedback profiles reflect the online reputation of both the buyers and sellers. When any transaction is complete both sellers and buyers are invited to rate how successful it has been and leave

41

a review. These reviews can be read by all users. eBay's online payments system PayPal is offered as a secure service which instantly transfers payments from one member's account to another without having to reveal any banking or credit-card details.

THE NEW-MEDIA ERA OPERATING UPSIDE DOWN

'Among our newspapers as they now stand, little more can be said in their favour than that they do not require batteries to operate, or can swat flies with them, and they can still be used to wrap fish.'

JOSEPH EPSTEIN, Commentary

The dearth of the passive audience

Marketing today is undergoing some significant evolution. In fact everything in this world is being turned upside down in that one of the most significant changes has been in the role of the consumer, which is shifting from one of passive recipient (e.g. television, magazines, billboards and newspapers) to a role with greater interaction. Today the recipients have more power to influence what they want to see or listen to. Although marketing has tried to ride this shift by moving advertising online, studies have shown that users just close or disable pop-up dialogues or just ignore what is not of interest to them. Online advertising leaves less of an imprint on the recipient than what the ads do on the TV and other passive media. For example try and remember an advert you saw when you last logged in, then try and remember an advert you saw on television the last time you switched it on.

What is positive for those wanting to market goods and services is that it is becoming easier to target consumers more directly based upon what they do online. For example if you Google for a 'holiday home in Cornwall', it is possible that you could also be interested in hearing about holiday homes in Devon and may also be interested in special offers, e.g. a timeshare. Hence related adverts will appear that you could find of genuine interest, which would not be possible using passive media such as the television. In the UK the introduction of the Phorm system (see Chapter 5) by three of the main broadband providers is going to make this even more evident and we discuss this in detail later.

The approach to market research is changing, embracing the vibrant voices of the web in a bottom-up manner. One of the things that makes the web so appealing is that for any subject, no matter how obscure, there is almost guaranteed to be at least one website, blog or discussion forum where people are meeting and talking about it. The internet's oldest discussion system, called Usenet, dates back to 1979 and can now be easily reached via Google which also maintains archives of discussions going back 25 years. Most of these discussions are of little interest except to their participants, however the direct and unfiltered nature of the content of online discussions is gold dust to large companies that want to spot trends or find out what customers really think of them. As a result many companies now monitor online conversations in addition to following those more traditional forms of marketing. There are some small specialist firms in existence today that are using a combination of computers and human researchers to track general discussions and try to spot trends early, by identifying members of the online communities who are most likely to influence other participants. This form of market research has significant differentiators to the more traditional form: (1) opinions appear on the web within minutes of an event, a market survey in contrast can take weeks or months; (2) participants in discussion groups can say anything they like, whereas in a market survey they only answer questions that the researchers think to ask.

Downloads are transforming the music business and pay-per-view for movies and cable TV, while advertising is migrating to the internet. The rules of media advertising have changed: favourites on where to spend money are Google and Yahoo! at the expense of large conglomerates. As with the media revolution of 1448, the wider implications for society will become visible gradually over a period of decades. Corporations today have to be part of the conversation. They have no choice as the alternative is that the people of the rest of the world will just continue without them. This has profound implications for the traditional business models in the media industry, which are based on aggregating large passive audiences and holding them captive during advertising interruptions. A passive audience has evolved into an active participant; the combined voice of a number of active participants has the power to influence the success or failure of any new product or service being launched.

Participatory media taking part in the conversation

'Young readers don't want to rely on a god-like figure from above to tell them what's important, and to carry the religion analogy a bit further they certainly don't want news presented as a gospel. What newspapers need to do online to adjust is to become a place for conversation. The digital native doesn't send a letter to the editor anymore. She goes online and starts a blog. We need to be the destination for those bloggers.'

RUPERT MURDOCH, chairman of News Corporation

The media of the new era is hence known as participatory media. The consequences of participatory media are that the boundary between the audience and creator has become blurred and often invisible, as participatory media are 'conversations' among the people formerly known as the audience. The conversations are open-ended and assume equality.

Newspapers that are successful are those that are becoming part of the conversation and those are the newspapers that have websites with content that is free or mostly free allowing bloggers to link in the articles to their sites.

Those blogs that are good normally link with other blogs that are good and even though many are amateur they are nonetheless smarter than the professional journalists because of a possession of specialist knowledge or expertise. Unlike journalists most bloggers do little or no original reporting, but they do post their opinions online. Opinions are easy to voice and are cheap, unlike traditional news gathering.

> 'Journalism is like making beer. Without formal training and using cheap equipment, almost anyone can do it. The quality may be variable, but the best home-brews are tastier than the stuff you see advertised during the Super Bowl. This is because big brewers, particularly in America, have long aimed to reach the largest market by pushing bland brands that offend no one. The rise of home-brewing has however forced them to create "micro-brews" that actually taste of something. In this same way bloggers have shaken up the mainstream media.'
>
> GLENN REYNOLDS, *An Army of Davids*,
> Thomas Nelson, 2006

In South Korea, OhmyNews changed the South Korean politics and media market with its online newspaper and the most successful example of 'citizen journalism' found in April 2006. OhmyNews has no reporters on its staff, instead it relies on amateurs or citizens, as Mr Oh (the founder and boss) prefers to call them. The OhmyNews website has a 'tip-jar' system that invites readers to reward good work with small donations. All they have to do is click a tip-jar button to have their mobile phone or credit-card account debited. OhmyNews also has a built-in feedback and rating system so that the best articles rise to the top. OhmyNews was originally set up as a not-for-profit company but since 2003 has turned into a for-profit company (The Economist 2006b). It also makes money from advertising and syndication revenues (from other internet sites that run OhmyNews's articles). The ramifications for South Korea's media industry are that they have been forced to adjust to the model used by OhmyNews.

Yahoo! provides a good example of the mixing of professional and amateur content. Many of the articles, photos, audio and video come from corporate partners, such as Associated Press, CNN etc. and some come from Yahoo! itself, and increasingly content is coming from the Yahoo! users. Yahoo! explicitly allows users not only to contribute content but also take part in its filtering and placement. Some well-publicised examples of user-created content in action are the terrorist attacks on the London Underground in 2005. Quite a few people took photos of the resulting chaos with their mobile phones that they wirelessly uploaded to Flickr (a photo-sharing site owned by Yahoo!). Others then tagged these photos by attaching labels such as 'London Underground' or 'bombings' to them so that they could be easily found. The pictures were then rated by visitors. This in turn brought the best pictures to the attention of Yahoo!'s human editors, who displayed them alongside professional content across Yahoo!'s news sites. All of this happened within minutes! These new collaborative processes have been named 'folksonomies' to distinguish them from the traditional top-down 'taxonomies' that human editors create.

'The obvious benefit of this media revolution is that we are entering an age of cultural richness and abundance of choice that we've never seen before in history. Peer production is the most powerful industrial force of our time.'

CHRIS ANDERSON, editor of *Wired Magazine*

3 Having Fun Safely Online: Some Golden Rules

Blogging should be fun and anyone can be a blogger, although you should be aware of some 'golden rules' for online communications, and you should be aware of these before you start to share, to be a part of 'the conversation'. This chapter attempts to clarify things for you.

YOUR IDENTITY, PRIVACY AND YOUR REPUTATION

Just as public spaces have many purposes in social life, they allow people to make sense of the social norms that regulate society, they let people learn to express themselves and learn from the reactions of others and they let people make certain acts or expressions 'real' by having witnesses acknowledge them (Boyd 1998), social networking sites are yet another form of public space. However while the mediated and unmediated public play similar roles in people's lives, Boyd (2007a) has defined that the mediated public have four properties that are unique to them:

- *Persistence.* What you say sticks around. This is great for asynchronous communication, but it also means that what you said at 15 is still accessible when you are 30 and have purportedly outgrown your childish ways.
- *Searchability.* Today's teens can be found in their hangouts with the flick of a few keystrokes by concerned parents.
- *Replicability.* Digital bits are copyable; this means that you can copy a conversation from one place and paste it into another place. It also means that it is difficult to determine whether the content has been doctored.

- *Invisible audiences.* While it is common to face strangers in public life, our eyes provide a good sense of who can overhear our expressions. In mediated public not only are lurkers invisible, but persistence, searchability and replicability introduce audiences that were never present at the time when the expression was created.

In this space you can build an online reputation that can be negative (as is mainly publicised by the popular media) or positive.

> 'That's how it was for us at Digital Equipment already 25 years ago. We had our forums in VAX notes, a Digital developed forum software, that we took great pride in. Its initial implementation was inspired by the notes functionality in the PLATO system, a legendary teaching system developed at the Urbana campus of the University of Illinois. The creator of the first Notes version within Digital was Len Kawell (1978 or there abouts), who I'm pretty sure had firsthand experience of PLATO. He later went on to create Lotus Notes with Ray Ozzie, Tim Halvorsen et al. In VAX Notes we used to share ideas and thread our interactions, a form of brain-storming and mutual support, we even discussed our hobbies in forums dedicated to topics covering most things between gardening and curling.[2] We built up virtual relationships within Digital, even if we had never met. We made virtual friends, and over time developed "on-line reputations". All of this happened within our workplace, hence our 'online reputations' normally had an impact on our professional reputation, and this felt good.'
>
> KJELL ÖSTMAN, former employee of
> Digital Equipment, now at HP

It has become usual for today's recruitment agencies to 'Google' applicants during the screening process and some of us do the same when we meet somebody new. Surveys (Madden et al. 2007) have highlighted that a significant number of internet users have 'Googled' for information on someone that they know, have known or are dating.

As the popularity of social networking sites has increased the previously distinct line between the workplace and private persona has become somewhat distorted. For example potential employers are starting to check a job candidate's online profiles on social networking sites prior to extending an offer of employment. Any pictures depicting a potential employee engaged in personal activities such as drug use, drinking or sexual exploits may harm that candidate's chances of future employment. Similarly pictures or videos of employees acting inappropriately can lead to a damaged reputation of the affected government or organisation, which is exactly what happened in October 2007 when Canada Border Services Agency officers were accused of posting inappropriate and offensive material, some of it directly related to their jobs, on the internet (CBC News 2007). On the other hand a good online reputation can enhance your physical persona. Having a good online reputation can be rewarding. A nice example of this is given above by Kjell Östman who today works for HP.

Tip: 'Google' yourself regularly, you may be surprised at what you find.

What you do online will inevitably over time enable you to build one or more online identities. Thus whether you are online as yourself or under a pseudonym you will inevitably over time build one or more online reputations. There is a distinct relationship between your identity and reputation since, first, what we do in our real physical life has an impact on our reputation (professional, personal etc.) and, second, it is by building our reputation that we create for ourselves an identity. Clearly as any individual may have many virtual identities, it is highly probable that a portion of these could present some linkage to their physical identity. Any information that you share or post will quickly become 'digital information residue'. Digital information residue is personal information that has been collected or shared and digitally stored somewhere by someone or something in cyberspace.

This brings to mind some questions concerning our identity (Öqvist 2007a). What is our identity? Are we at threat of losing control of whom we are or whom we are perceived to be? Are there not parts our lives that we would prefer not to have recorded digitally for prosperity? If our virtual identities become linked to our physical identities, what are the consequences? Is it possible that whatever we do as our virtual identities can influence decisions that other people make about us in the physical world? In effect does this mean that personal or sensitive information found on the internet has the potential to be damaging to what any one of us wants to achieve today or tomorrow?

Online adults can be divided into four categories based on their level of concern about their online information and whether or not they take steps to limit their online footprint (PEW Internet and American Project, see http://pewresearch.org/pubs/663/digital-footprints).

1. **Confident creatives** are the smallest of the four groups, comprising 17% of online adults. They say they do not worry about the availability of their online data and actively upload content, but still take steps to limit their personal information. Young adults are most likely to fall into this group.

2. The **concerned and careful** fret about the personal information available about them online and take steps to proactively limit their own online data. One in five online adults (21%) fall into this category.

3. Despite being anxious about how much information is available about them, members of the **worried by the wayside** group do not actively limit their online information. This group contains 18% of online adults.

4. The **unfazed and inactive** group is the largest of the four groups: 43% of online adults fall into this category. They neither worry about their personal information

nor take steps to limit the amount of information that can be found out about them online.

The fact is that any information that we post online even in its unstructured format can be linked directly to our identity if we choose and often even when we do not. Not all online activities that are digitally preserved are linked to our physical identity especially if we are using a pseudonym, but some could have a 'dormant identity linkage', i.e. a link that is not an obvious link but becomes active as a result of the following.

- Another physical identity's knowledge of specific personal information about the person (e.g. a name change), hence the aggregate of knowledge leads to identity linkage and exposure that would not have otherwise been possible (largely because aggregations of data may be more sensitive than the individual items alone).

- Personal information that is shared under an alias could be contaminated because within the same space there are links to their physical identity, i.e. in their 'friends list' are 'real physical' friends that know their real name.

The theme that presents itself repeatedly is the possible linkage between our online activities and our physical identity and the potential impact our online activities could have on our physical identity or reputation. In this book we call this the 'identity linkage continuum'.

> 'More than half of all employers use some kind of online screening technology including social networking sites like Facebook and MySpace.'
>
> NATIONAL ASSOCIATION OF
> COLLEGES AND EMPLOYERS (NACE)

The 'Janus Identity Model' in Figure 3.1 presents the concept of the identity linkage continuum, showing the physical and online identities or shadow reflecting each other on a timeline and the time is today. The online activities are somewhere

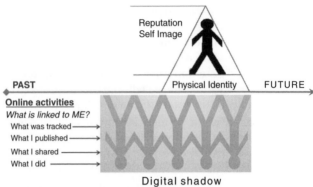

FIGURE 3.1   *The Janus Identity Model (Öqvist 2007a)*

in the past, which could be a measurement of seconds, minutes or years, and they have the potential to have an impact on an individual's physical identity today. The residue (information that is floating out there somewhere in cyberspace) of online activities is timeless and hence can have an impact, either positively or negatively, on an individual's reputation in the real world regardless of where on the timeline the physical identity is situated. The assumption is that most online activities are at sometime linked to an online identity, whether this is an alias, real name, email address etc.

> 'Identity Linkage Continuum denotes a many-to-one relationship between an individual's online activities and physical identity. The identity linkage is not affected by time and may comprise of positive or negative influences on an individual's physical identity/reputation at any given time during their life.'
>
> ÖQVIST, 2007a

The model is named after the Roman mythological god Janus, the god of gates, doors, doorways, beginnings and endings, and also known for his namesake, the month of January.

This identity model, similar to the god Janus, is depicted with two faces looking in opposite directions, originally represented the Sun and the Moon, but on this model representing the physical and the virtual world.

Similarly to this 'Janus identity model' the god Janus was frequently used to symbolize change and transitions such as the progression of past to future, of one condition to another or of one vision to another.

The control that we have over our identity today influences how we are perceived by our friends, employers, colleagues and those individuals that we have not yet had the pleasure of meeting. It also has an impact on how we are perceived as individuals in the future. This is nothing new except when we consider that often what we do today is stored in digital format somewhere by someone or something. The consequences can be positive and negative. It is positive if it reaffirms what you have stated about yourself. If it is something that you would prefer to forget, then you could have a problem.

THE RIGHT TO ANONYMITY AND PSEUDONYMITY ONLINE

The moral and ethical issues of anonymity

There are strong moral and ethical issues that surface when you talk about the right to remain anonymous. In fact the right to anonymity is to a certain extent the invention of our modern era. Anonymity in the village environment of old times was unheard of and this is why anonymity was one of the attractions of living in the town. It felt good to be unknown and unnoticed by the crowds, to experience that strangely liberating feeling after years of life in a small town or village where everyone knows everything about everyone else.

Anonymity grants us a freedom to 'speak our minds' in a way that we may not normally do because it may go against what is understood as the social norm. In fact 'freedom of speech' would not be possible in some situations without the cloak of anonymity. To be able to speak anonymously may sometimes be needed, particularly in suppressive regimes.

Today in the information society, the choice to be anonymous is disappearing. For example nowadays before we make that phone call we need to think if we want the caller to know who has tried to ring them if they do not answer. The recipient on the other hand has the choice to reject those calls that they do not feel like taking based on the name displayed on the telephone. Hence in this example the recipient of the call is given more information to make a quality choice by removing that cloak of anonymity that the caller used to have until they spoke.

Online, the right to anonymity in some countries is banned or severally restricted (Privacy International 2006a). Even in those countries where it is permitted, in reality absolute untraceable online anonymity is almost impossible. If someone wants to and has the authoritative powers and resources to trace you, they will find you, although this means that they may need to have the support of local government, supporting legislation and international cooperation. An example of a true story can be found in the book 'The Cookoo's Egg', Stoll (2000). It is entertaining reading even for those technophobes among us: it gives us some insight into how a hacker was traced even though he was using aliases, as hackers are prone to do.

A right for anonymity?
- In Bulgaria, identity cards are required to access cybercafés and internet service providers have to register the ID numbers of users.
- Individuals in France must be identifiable whilst online if they wish to publish content.
- The Italian council of ministers is approving a law requiring every blogger to register with the state.

(Continued)

(Continued)

- The Israeli government has proposed biometric authentication of adults wishing to view pornographic, violent or gambling content online.
- In Singapore ID is required when using an internet service provider (ISP).
- All service providers in South Africa must gather detailed personal data on individuals before signing contracts or selling SIM cards.
- ID is required in Thailand to buy SIM cards.

Although we cannot expect to receive absolute anonymity online, anonymity can be used as a tool to provide a cloak of privacy to selected online activities. For those countries where online anonymity is restricted or banned, it should still be possible to participate in forums anonymously unless access to these forums is blocked. The remainder of this section provides some tips on anonymity and when you may find it useful.

Tip: To keep your profile really anonymous avoid adding any 'friends' that are also your real friends in the physical world or 'friends' that know your real name. They may make a posting in their blog that reveals your real identity.

If you have a unique alias 'Google' it occasionally to check that nobody that you actually know has linked you into their friends list or permalinked one of your posts.

Pseudonyms and aliases

Fortunately most of us are not hackers or criminals and therefore not of enough interest to track down. So the use of pseudonyms and aliases enable us to effectively act anonymously in the online communities. Anonymity is a great way to express your opinions online whilst keeping the risks associated with your online activities to a minimum, i.e. without revealing your identity, damaging your reputation and losing your privacy. To be anonymous online you should have no personal information related to yourself in your profile that you have created for your social networking account or blog and what you do have there should be false.

Tip: Have you thought of keeping a separate email address for online activities on untrusted sites and what about a separate credit card (with a lower credit limit) just for those online transactions?

Anonymity online can empower participants of forums to contribute without needing to be accountable for their actions, which may otherwise have an impact on their online and offline reputation. In addition anonymity online gives people who may otherwise be inhibited the opportunity to communicate in a way that they have never done before. This may lead to increased self-confidence as well as giving them increased satisfaction and development potential in their physical life. Often a person that chooses to act anonymously will adopt a pseudonym. A pseudonym enables the linkage of different messages from the same person and thereby the maintenance of a long-term relationship under the pseudonym. Communication that is linked to a pseudonym can be classified as pseudonymous. To participate in an online forum (e.g. Yahoo Groups) as anonymous you first need to create an email account using any alias ID that does not have any relation to your real name and then use the alias to participate in the forums. Do not make any reference to real places or people's names that you know, as this provides a dormant linkage to your identity that can be used to work out who you are. You need to be very strict at keeping your pseudonym separate from your real identity to be successful at remaining anonymous over long periods of time.

Online fraud and SPAM

Have you noticed how your mailbox keeps filling up with SPAM? Where is it coming from? Well there is a whole army of 'botnets' out there programmed to send SPAM to every email address that they have harvested from somewhere. As long as you are online you will be a victim of SPAM. You can minimise the risk with a 'defence in depth' strategy, i.e. ensuring you have antivirus software on your PC that is checking for malware (malicious code) and then SPAM filtering solutions implemented to filter out the worst of the SPAM, a service that should be available from your email provider.

Furthermore spammers will try and harvest any information they can from these social networking and blog sites, so avoid posting email addresses in clear text. There are some javascripts available that enable you to post email addresses without this risk. Another approach is to use 'at' instead of the '@' sign in email addresses, e.g. firstname.lastname AT domainname dot com.

Tip: When sending emails to groups of people, create groups in whichever email program you are using. This gives some anonymity to the recipients and protection against programs collecting email addresses out there for the purpose of SPAM; even the recipients themselves cannot see who else got the email, although the name of the group may give an indication.

It is also quite smart to create alias email addresses (that are free, e.g. Yahoo, Hotmail) just for those online activities whereby you are not 100 per cent sure that you trust the site.

Tip: If you do not know who sent you an email delete it. Do not open, respond or click on any link contained within it. Remember to empty your email trash regularly.

Although this is outside the scope of anonymity for this section, it is worth noting that you can take the same approach with your credit card for online purchases. Have one credit card for online purchases with a low credit limit and keep online purchases completely separate from the card that you normally use offline or on trusted sites. It does not eliminate the risk of fraud on your credit card, but does at least provide you with some security by reducing the scale of potential fraud as a result of online transactions. The use of services such as PayPal is also gaining popularity. PayPal acts as a sort of proxy for you, thus instead of you leaving your credit card details at every site where you complete an online purchase you instead pay PayPal and they complete the payment transactions for you.

Anonymous storage

Freenet allows the creation of private encrypted networks for storage of content. It is very pro-anonymity, pro-privacy, pro-free speech. The system basically allocates a chunk of hard drive space from everyone participating in the network. The content of Freenet is encrypted and stored in this large distributed database made up of all of these different computers. They have just added some technology to allow standard internet-style bulletin board communications where people are able to have threaded discussions with complete assured anonymity and an inherent database, which is what any kind of a discussion board requires, absolute encryption and no ability to trace who sees what.

However it does mean that as a participant in this network you have no idea how your hard drive is being used. It could literally just be storing free speech articles on governments or actions somewhere in the world, but at the same time it could be something that you find distasteful such as pornography or even worse illegal such as child pornography.

Anonymised surfing

Anonymizer.com is an anonymising service that has been around for at least a decade. It will allow you to anonymously acquire information, in other words it will allow you to anonymously surf the internet so that you go to sites that have no idea who you are. However as already mentioned earlier in this section these types of service cannot give absolute anonymity. The service is based on using something called a 'proxy' that 'hides' your IP address from the rest of the world. It does not stop someone in authority with appropriate powers from accessing this service directly. From the proxy they will be able to pull out a list of all IP addresses that are using this service and this unique IP address will link back to your ISP and then to your PC.

The Onion Router (Tor)

Tor is a system that enables its users to communicate anonymously on the internet through a massive network of onion router nodes, and it is quite effective! Users create a connection through this network to a remote server; this could be for web surfing, sending messages, email or whatever. Tor is a network of virtual tunnels and works by distributing your communications across several places all over the internet, thereby making it more difficult to track you down. The originator of a connection chooses at random some number of onion routers that are in the network and there are nearly 1,000 of them scattered across the globe. By using 'layers' of encryption (hence the use of the term 'onion'), anonymity for the sender is made possible.

There is a great podcast from Steve Gibbons that gives a deep insight into the workings of Tor at http://www.grc.com/SecurityNow.htm (search on the page for 'Tor').

TAKING CONTROL OF YOUR IDENTITY

So now you are a virtual entity. You have a blog joining the ranks of those four out of ten Britains, one of the 17 per cent in France, 12 per cent in Germany or wherever you happen to live. In the online world you are keeping in touch with your friends on social networking spaces such as Facebook, Bebo and MySpace. Maybe you even have a Second Life. Throwing caution to the wind you are starting to have fun online.

In April 2007 market-research firm Gartner predicted that by the end of 2011, 80% of active internet users will have some sort of presence in a virtual world, with Second Life currently one of the most populous . . .

So hang on a moment before you get carried away: take the time to read this section on taking control of your identity and privacy, before it takes control of you. Think about what you are doing. Anything you post online becomes public immediately.

First advice, 'Google' yourself and see what is returned in the search result. If the result is unexpected and presents a threat to your physical (or online) reputation then contact a company such as ReputationDefender. Be aware that even if you have not posted anything online on yourself, someone else may have done so.

ReputationDefender (http://www.reputationdefender.com) is an example of a business that specialises in eradicating digitally stored information residue that could be personally damaging to your reputation. Their goals are straight-forward:
- to SEARCH and document digitally stored information residue in cyberspace wherever it may be;
- to DESTROY at the customers' request all inaccurate, inappropriate, hurtful and slanderous information using their in-house developed products.

Their services include those targeted at parents that want to be kept informed of any digital residue that can be found online on their children.

Taking control of your online identity is a challenge that many of today's younger generation are beginning to appreciate as they join the workforce and forge a career sometimes in areas that require impeccable background checks. It would be no surprise if the future were to bring a rapid growth in those businesses specialised in hunting down and eradicating digitally stored information residue that could be linked to us, as young people start to realise that something that they have published, shared or have done in the past online might have an impact on their professional or personal prospects in the physical world.

There are always two sides to the coin and in the information society professional networking has reached new heights. In this world we use a search engine to track our digital footprints. We are not playing at social networking; we are doing it to market ourselves professionally, to build our reputation. We have created personal profiles and linked with other professionals based on the assumption of mutual trust and personal recommendations.

Just as your curriculum vitae presents a resumé of your qualifications and experience in the real world, your online personae is used to market yourself professionally in the online world. Within your profile will be listed your 'contacts' as opposed to 'friends' in social networking. The 'old school network' has become unfettered by society conventions. Membership requires linking with reservations, i.e. not in promiscuous mode as is common in online social networking. You add someone to your personal network on the assumption that you either know them personally or they have been referred by someone you trust. Linking *ad-hoc* would reduce the credibility of your profile (except in special examples such as in the case of head-hunters that act as a hub, similar to Fakesters in the social networking space).

How much personal information you include in your profile is determined by the need to provide enough information to network effectively and, on the other side of the coin, keeping personal content to a minimum, since it is made public to everyone in your 'contacts' list. In the most popular professional networks you have the choice to keep the details of your 'contacts' list hidden.

With millions of connected professionals recommending each other it is a gold mine for new business opportunities, searching for new job opportunities, posting jobs and finding high-quality passive candidates for unadvertised roles. An example of a power-user of these professional online communities is the head-hunter.

LinkedIn (http://www.linkedin.com) is an online network of more than 17 million experienced professionals from around the world, representing 150 industries. When you join, you create a profile that summarises your professional accomplishments. Your profile helps you find and be found by former colleagues, clients and partners. Your network consists of direct connections (those that you know and trust), two degrees (those that are friends of friends) and three degrees (their friends). Your total network grows exponentially with every new connection.

There are companies around that are providing services to help us manage our online identities or to give us the ability to regain control of our identities. For example ZoomInfo is a business information search engine, with profiles on more than 37 million people and 3.5 million companies. ZoomInfo delivers unstructured information in a structured way. In fact it does more than LinkedIn which is focused on professional networking. For example it searches the internet for occurrences of your name in newspapers published around the world. If instances are returned you are given the option to claim them as linked to your identity. To prove your identity you need to provide your credit-card details. Once you have claimed your identity, any person that Googles you will be returned with your ZoomInfo profile near the top of the search ranking. The main benefit of this tool is that it gives you the ability to have some control on what you want people to find on you first.

'When psychotherapist Andrew Feldmar was travelling to the US from Canada in the summer of 2006, he probably expected some stringent checks at the border. In the wake of 9/11, entering the United States has not been a trivial matter; foreign nationals are often kept waiting in

(Continued)

(Continued)

line for over an hour while detailed questions, searches and background checks are carried out. Homeland security is a national priority, after all, and an insecure border poses an unacceptable threat.

What Feldmar wasn't expecting, though, was that one of those background checks would involve an internet search on his name. Among the search results was an article that Feldmar had written in 2001 for a psychiatric journal, relating his experiences in the 1960s with hallucinogenic drugs.

Despite having crossed the border more than 100 times since he'd stopped experimenting with drugs, Feldmar was told by a security guard that as a former drug user, he was no longer welcome in the United States. His fingerprints were taken, and he was turned back to Canada. In a subsequent interview with the *International Herald Tribune*, Feldmar said: "I should warn people that the electronic footprint you leave on the net will be used against you. It cannot be erased".'

PAUL JOHNS, Anti-social networking,
http://www.bcs.org, November 2007

GET TO KNOW YOUR BLOGGING CODE OF CONDUCT

As the blogosphere grows the junction between blogging about work and blogging in general grows murkier. The lack of legal guidance has forced some employers to fire employee bloggers for postings of a non-work nature on personal blogs, out of a fear that employees will divulge confidential information or speak ill of the company online. Other employers either ban the use of personal blogs completely or adopt blogging guidelines. My employer Hewlett-Packard have adopted a blogging guideline, so if you visit my blog (http://mysecuritybox. blogspot.com) you will find a disclaimer (Figure 3.2) that

DISCLAIMER

I am a Security Solution Architect
with Hewlett-Packard. The
postings on this blog reflect only
my personal views; they do not
necessarily represent the views,
positions, strategies or opinions of
HP or its management.

FIGURE 3.2   *The HP employee
blogging disclaimer*

links through to the HP webpage on the 'HP Blogging Code of
Conduct' (http://www.hp.com/hpinfo/blogs/codeofconduct.
html).

HP and many other technology companies can even go as
far to say that they support blogging activities. They understand the power of the voice of their workforce. Many are
adopting the practice of hosting an internal blog space (on
the intranet) and some companies may also have a web page
dedicated to employees that are bloggers in the public
domain, as is done by HP and shown in Figure 3.3. However
when I post public I need to be careful that I do not share
anything that is confidential to HP. To ensure that nothing is
posted by accident, which is difficult when you have interesting
work, I avoid posting about my work with HP or my personal
opinions on the workplace etc.

Keep your passwords safe

Keep your passwords safe and do not tell them to
anyone. Change them occasionally, try and use a combination of letters and numbers, and avoid using a password that is based on any personal details that you have
provided in your profile or that you have posted in your
blog.

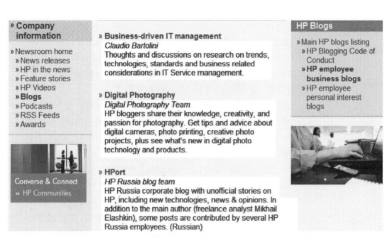

FIGURE 3.3   *HP website publicises HP employees' blogs*

However there are cases in some companies of employee bloggers that have been fired and have had no legal redress. Even though these cases are more prevalent in the United States, there are also cases in Europe. A turning point for bloggers was that of a British expatriate living in France who was fired for authoring an anonymous personal blog, however a French court ruled in her favour. She was the second British citizen fired for blogging (Privacy International 2006a).

YOUR PROFILE

Whether you are creating a blog or creating a profile in a social networking space, the first thing that is required is to create a profile. This profile includes information about your demographics and tastes, a self-description and often a photo. When creating the profile you should keep the following points in mind.

1. How much information do you want to share? Remember there are no laws to protect information that you share on yourself online in social and professional networking spaces.

2. If you are a minor, you should ask your parents/ guardians advice before loading a picture of yourself online. Ask them to read this book first.
3. Be aware that there are people out there who are more interested in you than you are in them.
4. Consider using a pseudonym, especially if you are a minor. Why not set up a Fakester, it could prove to be quite fun, e.g. a chronicle in the life of your dog or your cat.
5. Avoid including demographics on yourself. Those experienced in online data-mining may be able to find you in the real world. In worst-case scenarios women can become a victim to stalkers and children to paedophiles etc.
6. Always keep in mind that the more information you share on yourself the more vulnerable you make yourself to identity fraud (theft).
7. Keep your passwords safe and do not tell them to anyone. Change them occasionally, try and use a combination of letters and numbers, and avoid using a password that is based on any personal details that you've provided in your profile or that you have posted in your blog.
8. Try to keep your online life separate from your physical life. If you are a minor do not meet anyone that you have met virtually (online) alone. If you do want to meet someone take a friend or parent with you.

YOUR FRIENDS LIST AND PRIVACY SETTINGS

In blogging there are 'friends' and 'friends', but what does this mean?

Basically what it means is that you are tying in 'friends' with your privacy settings. So you can add your boss as a friend, but restrict them to the 'outer circle', i.e. they will

(Continued)

(Continued)

not be able to see everything that you do online that is only available to your 'inner circle' of online friends. In addition whoever you add to your 'outer circle' of friends has no way of knowing that they are not a part of the 'inner circle'. So you keep your boss happy as you accept their request as a 'friend' and you keep a level of privacy.

Social network sites also allow bloggers to publicly display their relations to each other, which in turn allows viewers to traverse the network. Once a user finds a profile of a friend (or anyone else) they can 'add' them. This sends a message to the other user requesting friendship; if the recipient approves the connection, the relationship is visible through both users' lists of friends.

By tying friendship to privacy settings, social networking sites encourage people to choose friends based on what they want to make visible. For example bulletins could be sent out to all friends informing them of changes to a profile. One typical change with younger bloggers is if they break up with their girlfriend or boyfriend when they change their status to 'single'.

For example if you have a Facebook profile and your boss Dave has added you to his friends list, the chances are that you do not want to upset Dave by ignoring his friend request. However you do not want to give Dave full access to your Facebook updates as he might soon work out, via your Facebook status for instance, that you are writing to your mum when you should be finishing that urgent report.

Accepting Dave as a friend but giving him access to only your limited profile in Facebook means that he will only see a tailored, cut-down version of your online information. In case you are wondering, when you set your boss up with your limited profile, he will not be aware of this, so whether you add Dave as a 'full' friend or a 'limited' friend, only you will know. Once you have added Dave as a friend, head to Facebook's privacy page and click limited profile. Put Dave's name in the box to limit his viewing to what you want, then hit the edit settings link to set what information you want to be made available.

Separate 'real' friends from 'online' friends

Teach your children to keep separate 'real-life friends' from 'online friends'. The rules you have for 'online friends' should be different from 'real-life friends'.

The number of friends one has affects the size of one's network, but connecting to collectors plays a significant role. Collectors can be visualised as 'social network hubs' as they have loads of friends that are not connected to each other. A collector can be a 'fake profile' (Fakester), i.e. the profile does not represent a real person. Examples of collectors include TV characters such as Homer Simpson, films and rock bands. Connecting people with shared interests facilitates networking between people with similar interests.

BLOGROLL, LINKING AND PERMALINKS

A typical blog does not have a 'friends' list as in the social networking spaces. Blogs have blogrolls, i.e. a list of blogs and bloggers that any particular blog author finds influential or interesting, so much so that the author wants the link to be enduringly visible on their site instead of just in occasional entries. A blogroll is often found on one side of a blog's entries and the hyperlinked names lead directly to the blogs in question. Blogrolls indicate which online community a blogger is attracted to or belongs to.

If you host a professional blog keep aware of who is linking into your blog. You could have a well-meaning friend or family member that has also created a personal blog giving a detailed chronicle of their life with your full name and hyperlink to your professional blog in their blogroll. Although clearly if the blog contains mundane, harmless content this may be fine, but on the other hand if the content is of an intimate nature it may be prudent to ask them 'very nicely' to remove the link. It is wise to try to keep your professional and private online activities separate. Why not send them a copy of this book, so that they will understand where you are coming from and not feel offended?

A hyperlink can be included in postings that you make on your blog and this is how it differs from a blogroll. A link from one posting to another helps provide context around an argument or point and it is essentially a 'vote of attention' from one blogger to another. By linking to another site, blog or profile the weblog author is saying 'I find what you are saying important enough to link to it'. Linking also helps create conversation and maintain context between blogs and individual postings.

The relevance of a site on the web can be determined by how often a source is cited and therefore considered an authority. Links in the world of weblogs are even more important since bloggers frequently link to and comment on other blogs, creating a sense of timeliness and back-and-forth one would have in a conversation. Technorati tracks the number of links and the unique source of links to determine the breadth and readership of any author or site.

Permalinks can be used in links. Permalinks are needed because the homepages of most weblogs have several entries or posts listed on them. As blogs tend to be frequently updated, articles you find on a weblog's homepage one day may not be there the next. A permalink is the permanent identifier to a specific posting or article. Bloggers love permalinks: they provide an easy way to capture specific references to posts or articles about which bloggers are writing.

POSTING, TAGGING AND RSS FEEDS

On your blog you will be having a conversation with whoever calls by. You will be excited when someone 'knocks on your door' leaving their calling card. You will soon find that your conversation becomes everyone's conversation. Conversations online have the ability to grow their own set of legs, with a tendency to move in unexpected directions. This is what makes blogging such fun!

Create a post on your blog

It is worth thinking twice before you post anything. If you post on a friend's wall, all of their friends and colleagues will be able to see what you have written, as well as the rest of the world if they have no privacy settings enabled. Therefore if you are writing anything personal or controversial, send this to them in a private message instead. Of course do not respond to someone else's personal message to you by writing back on their wall.

Avoiding online misunderstandings is an art

It is much easier to become offended online than it is offline. This is because online it is easy for the context of a posting to be lost. Understand that your audience is global: they will be from different cultures, backgrounds, religions and ages and also many of them may be using English as a second language.

Online misunderstandings are bound to happen, it is inevitable; it is not a matter of whether it will happen but a matter of when, and then how you handle it.

The best approach is to always assume that there has been a misunderstanding before taking any defensive stance. Respond to any aggression with calm. Keep your cool.

One golden rule in blogging is that you should not remove or change postings without leaving a clear trail. The reason is clear, as your postings maybe permalinked by other posts and these posts could lose their context if you remove or change the standpoint of your posting. Best blogging practices are that you should edit them to show that you have changed your opinion since you made the posting. This could be the result of a variety of reasons, such as new facts coming to light that make your previous posting an unfair judgement or maybe you are sorry that you managed to inadvertently offend one of your visitors. Figure 3.4 gives an indication of how you can handle any of these situations in a smart and polite way.

There are times when private messages are good ...

If you are writing a message to someone that contains anything that could be perceived as personal or controversial, send it directly to them in a private message. Of course if you receive a personal message yourself, respond with a personal message back.

So why is all this advice in a book on privacy? It is simple, if you start a heated discussion online and if the discussion is public it can have an impact on your reputation, not just online but in the physical world too, especially if your postings become really public. Think about what potential employers will find when they 'Google' your name.

I suppose the question is 'why would anyone want to do this'?. ~~Particularly in the case of Mark, seems like the guy had too much time on his hands. In fact~~ one of the most publicized areas is for the purpose of 'online grooming' of children by paedophiles. All of this subject area and more is covered in the book I expect to publish -once I decide who to publish with- in the next month or so. So watch this space :-)

FIGURE 3.4   *Example of a modified posting*
(from http://mysecuritybox.blogspot.com)

Also be aware that once you post information online, you lose ownership of that data. That data once posted 'belongs' to the website, not you. Whilst all reputable sites will publish a security and privacy policy, they all retain the right to change that policy at their discretion. In addition if they lose that data you have no right for redress.

Do not trust what other people post about themselves. It is very easy to lie about ourselves online. This also applies to reviews given online, whether they are about other bloggers or even books, restaurants or hotel reviews. There have been cases of people posting false reviews on themselves: it is online anonymity that makes this possible.

Tag your post

Once you create a post you can tag it. Tagging has emerged in 'social bookmarking' tools where the act of tagging a resource is similar to categorising personal bookmarks (Marlow et al. 2006). Tags allow you to store and collect postings and retrieve them using the tags applied. Figure 3.5 shows the tags applied to my blog, known as categories here. Every one of my posts is tagged as belonging to one or more of these categories, this makes it much easier for me to find content later on.

Keeping updated

So what do you do to keep updated on the latest postings on other blogs that are of interest to you? RSS is the answer. RSS is a family of web-feed formats used to publish frequently updated content such as blog entries, news headlines or podcasts. An RSS feed contains either a summary of content from an associated website or the full text. If you add an RSS feed to your blog, you will find a dynamic update on your blog of the latest postings from whichever blog the RSS is fed. So if you have an RSS feed to your favourite blog, newsfeed etc. everything that is posted on this blog will be presented as the title line of the posting in your blog, which you can click on if it is of interest to you, to be taken directly through to the post as a permalink. Then of course other bloggers that

CATEGORIES

- Attended Events and Notes (13)
- Censorship and Anonymity (1)
- Children (31)
- Cybercrime and Terrorism (6)
- LOL (12)
- My Publications (5)
- My Speaking Engagements (8)
- Out of the Box (65)
- Privacy (130)
- Publications and Speaking Engagements (8)
- Recommended Reading (11)
- Security (22)
- Surveillance (32)
- Virtual World and Gaming (21)
- Web 2.0 (53)

FIGURE 3.5   *Tags applied to a blog
(or categories)*

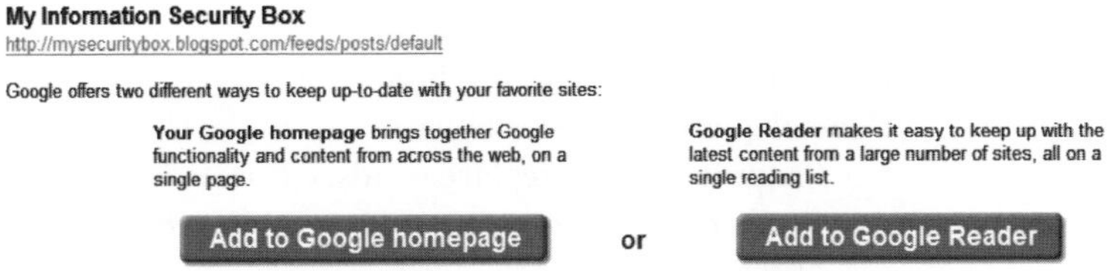

My Information Security Box
http://mysecuritybox.blogspot.com/feeds/posts/default

Google offers two different ways to keep up-to-date with your favorite sites:

Your Google homepage brings together Google functionality and content from across the web, on a single page.

Google Reader makes it easy to keep up with the latest content from a large number of sites, all on a single reading list.

Add to Google homepage   or   Add to Google Reader

FIGURE 3.6   *Creating an RSS feed*

find your blog of interest will create a feed of your postings to their blog.

RSS content can be read using software called an 'RSS reader', a 'feed reader' or an 'aggregator'. If we take the example in Figure 3.6, the user subscribes to a feed by entering the feed's link into the reader (shown as a hyperlink in the upper left-hand corner) or by clicking an RSS icon in a browser that initiates the subscription process. The reader checks the user's subscribed feeds regularly for new content, downloading any updates that it finds.

The hyperlink can also be fed into a mobile phone so you can pick up your RSS feeds while you are on the road.

LEARNING THE LINGO

AOL speak or internet slang

AOL speak, internet slang, txt or SMS is the English language slang used online and on mobile phone SMS. It is an abbreviated form of English similar to a rebus. (A *rebus*, from the Latin word meaning 'by things', is a kind of word puzzle which uses pictures to represent words or parts of words, for example Gr + 8 = Great.) The predictive text input functionality available in mobile phones has reduced its popularity, however it continues to be a most universal online language. It gives a median for people around the world, many of whom do not have English as their native language, the freedom to communicate simply and informally. Txt is a universal online language.

The objective of txt is to use the fewest characters needed to convey a comprehensible message. Hence punctuation and grammar are largely ignored much to the horror of most parents, grandparents and teachers.

General guidelines are as follows.

- Single letters can replace words, e.g. *cu = See you.*
- Single digits can replace words, e.g. *ate = 8, for = 4, to* or *too = 2.*
- Single letters or digits can replace a syllable, e.g. *Gr8 = great, b4 = before.*
- Miscellaneous abbreviations of words, removing unnecessary characters, e.g. *Sorry = sry, Tomorrow = 2moro.*

Online etiquette (netiquette)

There are many online rules quaintly termed as netiquette that are to a large extent followed, although less emphasis is placed on this today than a few years ago. This could be because people are becoming increasingly web-savvy in transferring what is logical in our physical world online. For example if we do not want to have bad language directed at us we should avoid using it ourselves. UPPERCASE online implies SHOUTING and emoticons are used to express emotions which help avoid misunderstandings; this can happen much easier when you are not engaging in face-to-face dialogue and are communicating in an international community.

Do not SHOUT!

Avoid using UPPERCASE when communicating online as this can be likened to SHOUTING.

Use emoticons ☺ as a means to put your messages into context, thus reducing the risk of misunderstandings.

Emoticons can be described best as 'laughter in cyberspace'. Since people cannot communicate sarcasm, teasing, humour or other emotions online, they use 'smileys' to convey these emotions. Some of the more popular smileys are listed in Table 3.1.

TABLE 3.1 *Smileys*

Smiley
\<g\> grin
:-) smiley face or ☺
;-) or ;-> a wink
:-(frown
:-P sticking out your tongue

Alternatively you can download some smileys in graphic format. Searching for 'smileys' in Google will bring up some results that look similar to the examples in Figure 3.7.

Some examples of chat abbreviations that you will commonly come across in your online communications are shown in Table 3.2.

Beware of trolls and flamebait

Other jargon known by online savvy users are those that refer to special behaviour online that could be used to incite

FIGURE 3.7   *A choice of fun smileys*

TABLE 3.2   *Chat abbreviations*

Chat abbreviations	
LOL	laughing out loud
FOFL	falling on the floor laughing
ROFLOL	rolling on the floor, laughing out loud
IMHO	in my humble opinion
PMJI	pardon me for jumping in

reactions from others or to deceive. Most commonly known are described in the Table 3.3.

YOU HAVE VISITORS

'Sometimes I wonder whether I care to the point that I neglect other things, like, oh, my job. Tweaking the blog is seductive in a way that a print deadline never is. By the time I am done posting entries, moderating comments and making links, my, has the time flown. I probably should have made some phone calls about next week's column, but maybe I'll write about, ah, blogging instead.'

Feedback through a fire hose,
http://www.bloggersblog.com/blogaddiction/

TABLE 3.3 *Beware of trolls and flamebait: online jargon*

Name	Description
Flaming	Beware of flaming which is the act of sending or posting messages that are deliberately hostile and insulting, usually in the social context of a discussion board on the internet. Do not allow yourself to be antagonised by them.
Troll	Beware of trolls: a troll is usually someone who enters an established community such as an online discussion forum and posts inflammatory, rude, repetitive, offensive, off-topic or otherwise disruptive messages designed intentionally to annoy or antagonise the existing members or alter the flow of discussion. Do not allow yourself to be one of them.
Flamebait	Avoid getting dragged into a flamewar as a result of flame-bait. A flamebait is a message posted to a public internet discussion group, such as a forum, newsgroup or mailing list, with the intent of provoking an angry response (a 'flamewar') or argument over a topic the troll often has no real interest in.
Sockpuppet	A sockpuppet is the additional account of an existing member of an internet community that is used to invent a separate user. This may be used for fictional support of people in a vote or argument by falsely using the account as a separate user or for acting without consequence to one's 'main' account. It is often considered dishonest by online communities and such pretending individuals are often labelled as trolls.

Once you have started your blog you will soon start obsessing over statistics such as how many visitors have been to your blog, how long did they visit for, where did they come from and where do your visitors live. This behaviour is fun and somewhat addictive. You start to think about how to increase visitors to your blog and how to make it more creative even when you are not online. You start to be 'permanently online' in that you see things in your real life and think 'I must write about this in my blog'.

You can see the demographics of who has been visiting your blog by imbedding a piece of code in your webpage from a service such as Google Analytics (http://www.google.com/analytics; see Figures 3.8–3.10). You will need to set up a profile with the URL of your blog. From here you will be provided with some tracking code that you need to embed

FIGURE 3.8   *Map overlay for Google Analytics*

```
<script type="text/javascript">
var gaJsHost = (("https:" == document.location.protocol) ? "https://ssl." : "http://www.");
document.write(unescape("%3Cscript src='" + gaJsHost +" google-analytics.com/ga.js'
type='text/javascript'%3E%3C/script%3E"));
</script>
<script type="text/javascript">
var pageTracker = _gat._getTracker("UA-1xxxxx9-2");
pageTracker._initData();
pageTracker._trackPageview();
</script>
```

FIGURE 3.9   *Google Analytics tracking code example*

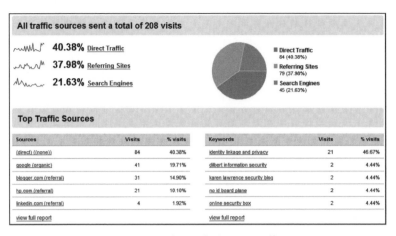

FIGURE 3.10   *Google Analytics top traffic sources*

between the <body> and </body> tags of the <html> code in your blog page. It sounds complicated but it is quite easy. There are plenty of help and tips at Google Analytics to help you start and troubleshoot.

This code will drop a cookie onto your visitors PC. From this you are able to determine not only their geography but also which network they use, how they arrived at your blog and also if they are new or a returning visitor. This enables you to ascertain visitor loyalty and understand better the impact it has when you post regularly and when you do not. It also keeps you motivated to keep posting when you see that someone actually likes to read what you post.

4 Your Children's Online Safety

PANDORA'S BOX

The virtual playground

So blogging is cool with Web 2.0 and all it represents, embracing collaboration and social networking. Web 2.0 is an enabler, making it so easy for us to share our personal information with the rest of the world, willingly and knowingly. This fact alone has opened a Pandora's box when it comes to our children's safety. Children like to show the world that they are here, what they do in their lives and what they think: they do not think twice about publishing photos and videos of themselves online and dating online is becoming the norm.

> 'If you're not on MySpace, you don't exist.'
>
> SKYLER, 18, to her mom
>
> 'I'm in the 7th grade. I'm 13. I'm not a cheerleader. I'm not the president of the student body. Or captain of the debate team. I'm not the prettiest girl in my class. I'm not the most popular girl in my class. I'm just a kid. I'm a little shy. And it's really hard in this school to impress people enough to be your friend if you're not any of those things. But I go on these really great vacations with my parents between Christmas and New Year's every year. And I take pictures of places we go. And I write about those places. And I post this on my Xanga. Because I think if kids in school read what I have to say and how I say it, they'll want to be my friend.'
>
> VIVIEN, 13, to Parry Aftab during a
> 'Teen Angels' meeting (Boyd 2007b)

In some countries there has been an enormous amount of publicity concerning the threats faced by children as internet users. In response to these growing problems legislation has finally been passed in some countries. However most of these threats are not unique to children: they apply to all of us. Two areas that are worth a special mention in this section are exposure to pornographic and violent web-content and online grooming leading to virtual or physical sexual abuse, which have been written with relevance to children in mind.

In fact the internet was originally designed by adults for adults, but in recent years there has been an invasion of children. The internet has provided children with a virtual playground that is not understood by adults nor policed by them. Hence there is no 'sandbox' within which it is safe to play. The internet is borderless: pornographic content made available on a server in Russia could be found by your children, and a paedophile living thousands of kilometres away could start a relationship with your child. What is more, all of this can happen whilst your children are sitting in the safety of their own home.

Exposure to pornographic and violent web content

The internet is full of pornographic and violent content. As a parent or guardian you may not see this as a significant threat because you will probably be using the internet for different things than what your children are. It is a fact that a high proportion of children and teenagers that use the internet regularly have a high probability of coming across sex-motivated sites either when searching for something else or receiving pornographic links and images via email. Also there is a significant proportion of children and teenagers that seek out these sex sites deliberately. To get an appreciation of what is out there you only need to 'Google' words such as 'girls', 'sex', 'penis', 'tsunami', 'massacre', etc., that is if you dare. These are the type of words that a teenager will most certainly 'Google' at some time.

Pornographic material

The internet has caused an explosive growth for the pornographic industry. There are hundreds of thousands of pornographic websites on the internet and this number is growing every day.

As children mature into adults and embark on the exciting journey of discovering their sexuality it is easy to see the internet as a fantastic resource on which to satisfy their curiosity. In general boys are more likely to search for pornographic content than girls and from this content they can form a picture on how the world is viewing sex, on how to treat girls, how their parents have sex and how normal people view sex and each other. In other words adolescents are absorbing this information and using it as a foundation for their base values upon which their sex life will be formed (Flood 2003).

Unfortunately in viewing internet pornography, children and adolescents are exposed to explicit images of a wide range of sexual acts. Most pornography centres on images of women's bodies and of male–female sexual activity and most is directed at a heterosexual male audience. Common pornographic material found on the internet includes practices such as kissing, sexual touching, masturbation, fellatio, vaginal intercourse, anal intercourse and much more.

There is very little direct research evidence to help understand the potential longer-term effects of this type of pornographic exposure on children. What some studies have indicated is that depictions of sexual behaviour may be emotionally disturbing to a child who encounters them, particularly with sexually explicit material that normally includes images or videos of non-mainstream behaviour. There is also the possibility that children that have continued exposure to images of non-mainstream sexual behaviour may be more likely to accept and adopt this behaviour themselves, having internalised this behaviour as normal. There is however no evidence to support this (Flood 2003).

Violent material

The type of content that can be found on the internet can be disturbing even for an adult. For example there are websites dedicated to the Asian tsunami of December 2004 depicting dead, bloated and rotting bodies.

Quite often boys are actively looking for these types of material and in general do not seem to be adversely affected by it, although there have been some studies indicating that regular viewing over long periods of time can cause a negative change in the way the child is acting or how they perceive the world. Girls tend to become upset or affected immediately and will normally inform their parents, particularly if they have problems sleeping and suffer nightmares as a consequence. Boys are not so forthcoming: they do not want to lose face in front of their peers.

Protecting your children: parental controls and tracking mechanisms

The Internet Content Resource Association (ICRA) has provided labels that are used to represent information about things that can be identified on the web and their suitability for children. Its predecessor was the Platform for Internet Content Selection (PICS).

Tip: If you feel you need to log your children's online activities it is good practice to show them what you are doing so there are no secrets and actually go through the log with them afterwards. When the day arrives that they ask that you remove the tracking, do so.

Software can be installed on a PC to restrict access to websites and chatrooms, blocking any pages that the parents consider as inappropriate. Parental controls allow the users to determine which rating services they want to use and, for each rating service, which ratings are acceptable and which are unacceptable. For example you might choose a rating service that rates documents according to their sexual content. The rating service might have a low rating for romance, a higher rating for passionate kissing and yet higher ratings for more explicit sexual activity. You might decide that documents containing romance are the highest acceptable rating for their household. You would then configure your browser to reject all documents that are unrated or contain a higher rating from this rating service. The main issue with parental controls is that when the settings are set too high, too many dialogs popup causing the child to just ignore them automatically. Feedback from some parents has been 'what a waste of time'.

If you have young children you may consider activating the tracking functionality that is included in parental control products. This will store a log of all of their online activities. This is quite invasive, but most parents have no qualms doing this with very young children. If you feel you need to do this, it is good practice to show them what you are doing so that there are no secrets and one day they will probably ask that you remove the tracking, in which case you should do so.

Tip: To get an idea of where your children have been online without feeling that you are invading your child's right to privacy, you can occasionally check their browsing history and check the source of any cookies that may have been downloaded onto the computer. Let your children see what you are doing, so there are no secrets.

Parental Controls in Windows Vista is a new tool built into the operating system that will not only let parents apply limits to the way their children can use the computer, but also has features tools that allow parents to keep track of what their kids are doing on the computer. What Microsoft has done is create a centralised location in Vista where you can find all of the family safety related settings. The end result is that you do not need to look in several places to find and configure these settings for your children: you can just go to one spot and configure everything from there. This includes restriction settings, where can your children go, and activity monitoring, what they have done online.

Paedophiles go online

'Child sexual assault and exploitation were once limited to physical locations such as school playgrounds, church vestibules, trusted neighbours' homes, camping trips and seedy, darkly lit back rooms of adult bookstores' (Ferraro and Casey 2005): a vision that conjures up the picture of a pae-dophile as a dirty old man, wearing a rain coat. This is an image that children have been spoon-fed for generations and which in truth does not reflect the reality because today's paedophile visits virtual social networking spaces rather than schools and playgrounds to find children to prey upon. By employing smart data-mining techniques the new-age paedophile can build up a detailed profile of their intended child victim and use this to win the trust of the child prior to any physical meeting, whilst also retaining anonymity.

In cyberspace paedophiles have created meeting places to exchange child pornography and tips on how and where to find victims, advice on successful 'grooming' techniques, methods of encryption and how to remain anonymous, basically fulfilling the role of what we would associate as a peer support group in the physical world. The impact of these groups is profound in that paedophiles are able to 'normalise' abnormal desires, enabling them to view their behaviour as socially acceptable and possibly lowering their inhibitions to act on impulses that would otherwise remain fantasy.

What's more the open nature of the internet has fuelled a brisk, multi-billion dollar trade in illicit material. While the exact relationship between the creation of child pornography and paedophile activity requires more research, the large volume of child pornography and child erotica trading online is viewed by some as physical evidence of paedophile activity and networking in the virtual world. Moreover, research has indicated that child pornography is regularly used by pae-dophiles as a means of desensitising children and normalising sexual activity between adults and children. ('Desensitising' in this context means that the child becomes familiar with sexual activity by viewing child pornography; often pictures can be of children involved in sexual activity and smiling, looking naturally happy and normal.)

Online grooming

'The process of "grooming" a child online involves deception techniques designed to lower the inhibitions of the child in order to exploit them sexually' (Brown 2001). The psychological methods of a paedophile are to induce a state of mind, affect the mind, cause moral offence or induce some action from the victim. They may achieve this by:

- masquerading as somebody younger than they really are;
- masquerading as somebody of a different gender;
- building trust by pretending to have the same interests, concerns etc. as the child;
- sharing secrets;
- using enticement and bribery;
- using emotional blackmail and intimidation techniques.

The Ideal Victim?

'Adolescents in general are more vulnerable than younger children because, in their typical quest for identity and independence, they are less apt to accept parental oversight. In addition, children with few friends or relatively little involvement in sports or other extracurricular activities are more likely to be vulnerable.'

DETECTIVE JAMES MCLAUGHLIN, Keene Police Department, http://www.ci.keene.nh.us/police/task_force.htm

The tactics employed are not new and have been used by social engineers for years to deceive victims into handing over money, information etc. Many offenders send pictures online to victims and send or offer gifts or money. Gifts can range from small tokens such as jewellery and teddy bears to expensive items such as clothing, mobile phones and digital cameras. Conversations about sex can happen during the first encounter or over a longer period of time if they are being 'groomed' for sexual exploitation. Paedophiles can also expose the victim to pornographic material during this period. The grooming of children over the internet by a paedophile has been defined as follows (O'Connell 2003): the friendship-forming stage, the relationship-forming stage, the risk-assessment stage, the exclusivity stage and the sexual stage. The details of these stages are given in Table 4.1.

TABLE 4.1   *The process of 'grooming a child online' (O'Connell 2003)*

Friendship-forming stage	In this stage the paedophile is getting to know the child. The length of time spent at this stage varies from one paedophile to another and the number of times this stage of the relationship is reenacted depends upon the level of contact the paedophile maintains with a child.
Relationship-forming stage	This is an extension of the friendship-forming stage and during this stage the adult may engage with the child in discussing, for example, school and/or home life. Not all adults engage in this stage but generally those who are going to maintain contact with a child will endeavour to create an illusion of being the child's best friend. More typically an initial relationship-forming stage will be embarked upon and then interspersed in the conversations will be questions that relate to the following risk-assessment stage.
Risk-assessment stage	A paedophile will ask the child about their environment, for example the location of the computer the child is

(Continued)

TABLE 4.1 *(Continued)*

	using and the number of other people who use the computer. By gathering this kind of information it seems reasonable to suppose that the paedophile is trying to assess the likelihood of his activities being detected by the child's parent(s), guardian(s) or older sibling(s).
Exclusivity stage	Here the tempo of the conversation changes so that the idea of 'best friends' or 'I understand what you're going through and so you can speak to me about anything' ideas are introduced into the conversation by the adult. The interactions take on the characteristics of a strong sense of mutuality, i.e. a mutual respect club comprised of two people that must ultimately remain a secret from all others. The idea of trust is often introduced at this point with the adult questioning how much the child trusts them and psychologically people, especially children, respond to this tactic by professing that they trust the adult implicitly. This often provides a useful means to introduce the next stage of the conversation, which focuses on issues of a more intimate and sexual nature.
Sexual stage	This stage can be introduced with questions such as 'Have you ever been kissed?' or 'Do you ever touch yourself?'. The introduction of this stage can appear innocuous enough because typically the adult has positioned the conversation so that a deep sense of shared trust seems to have been established and often the nature of these conversations is extremely intense.

The process of online grooming can have unexpected outcomes in addition to those of sexual abuse and child pornography, and that is that many victims in studies conducted were described as being in love with or having feelings of close friendship towards offenders. What this means is that the sexual abuse of a child could be considered at first as non-forcible crimes. In many cases child victims knew they were interacting with adults who were interested in them sexually. This has often presented difficulties in gaining support of law enforcement because the victim is unwilling to cooperate to capture the abuser.

Legislation protecting children from online abuse

An increasing number of countries today are enacting legislation to make 'online grooming' an offence. So the police have the tools to be able to protect online children as never before.

Proving that a child is being 'groomed' online and thus at risk in a court of law was impossible before 2003 in the UK unless some physical action was taken by the paedophile to meet the child and that the abuser was carrying sufficient evidence implying that sexual abuse would occur, e.g. condoms. In the UK the *Amendments to the Sexual Offences Act 2003 (s.15)* often referred to as the 'anti-grooming bill' corrected this discrepancy.

This need to protect children from 'grooming' by paedophiles that could ultimately lead to sexual abuse was addressed in these reforms to the *UK Sexual Offences Act 2003*. This act makes new provisions about sexual offences, their prevention and the protection of children from harm, sexual acts and connected purposes.

In addition the *Regulation of Investigatory Powers Act 2000* (RIPA) gives law enforcement agencies the tools to be more proactive in how they can detain offenders. This helps the law enforcement agencies, with the consent
(Continued)

(Continued)
of the child, to monitor or take over communications between the child and offender.

Other countries such as the United States and Australia have similar 'anti-grooming' laws in place. Some countries such as Sweden have filed proposals for the enactment of such a law, although this was in 2006, and the proposal was still not implemented by autumn 2008.

Not all cases of 'grooming' end up with sexual abuse of the child. For example it is often that the child feels uncomfortable with how the communication with the paedophile is developing and reports this to their parents, police or another adult; sometimes observant family members intervene before any meeting occurs and what is becoming very common is that many sex crimes are committed online, an example is that the paedophile persuades the child to send a pair of their underwear or they could get the child to send a sexually explicit video of themselves.

The use of webcams

Sexual abuse of a child can be both physical and virtual. On the section concerning paedophiles and how they desensitise children to becoming victims, we explained the 'grooming process' and one of these activities would be to encourage the child to take pornographic pictures of themselves and send them to the paedophile. The pictures can start off quite innocent and bit-by-bit become sexually explicit. This risk to the child rises considerably if the child has access to a webcam with the computer. The offender will encourage the child to take sexually explicit recordings of themselves which equates to virtual sexual abuse, which is treated as seriously as actual sexual abuse of a child. It could be that the risk is minimised if the only computer in the house is placed in a family area. However today children are often at home alone as it is normal for parents to be out at work.

The safest approach to dealing with this threat is to not have a webcam at home and this has been the most obvious advice given by those advocates of children's online safety. However as the computer evolves into a crucial part of a family's channel for communication, this approach is rapidly becoming obsolete, because it is no longer practical. After all a webcam can be a great tool for video conversations with grandma. Hence the only advice this book can offer is:

- be aware of the risks;
- make your children aware of the risks;
- make the decision yourself on whether you permit a webcam in your house or not.

Wish lists

It is not only paedophiles that present a threat to children, but also the children themselves. For example there is a trend that has emerged among teenage girls. 'Wish-lists' on home shopping sites enable teenagers to post what gifts they would most like, generally in exchange for posting revealing photos. There are thousands of such list registers with a turnover of millions of dollars annually. The teenage 'cam-girls' post photographs in their own blogs with the implication made of 'something more revealing' if a person sends them a present.

beAnonymous beSmart beSafe Online

This section provides a list of base rules that you can provide for your children to follow when in cyberspace. You should pin this or a similar list to the wall next to the computer. The main focus is on encouraging your children to play at being anonymous online and then to be smart about it. There are quite a few websites providing games and videos to help educate children about online safety. One of them is Kidsmart, hosted by Childsafe International (http://www.kidsmart.org.uk/); another is Safer Internet (http://www.safer-internet.net/).

beAnonymous

- **Create an 'online' fun name for yourself** for when you are online. You can be who you like.
- **Keep all information on your real self as a secret online**: never give away any information about yourself, including your name, address, name of your school, phone number etc. Even if someone tells you things about themselves, you cannot be sure that what they have told you is true.
- **Keep information about your parents and friends secret online**: never give you parents' names, friends' names, where your parents work, anyone else's email address or any telephone number to anyone you meet online.
- **Never show your picture online to someone** without your parents' consent.
- **Do not send anyone you meet online anything about yourself**.
- **Do not agree to meet with anyone you meet online** unless your parents agree and go with you.
- **Never give anyone you meet online your phone number**: be smart, if they insist, ask for their phone number and/or address and get your parents involved.
- **Do not accept anything from anyone you meet online**, including topping up money for your mobile phone, music etc. If they give you something they will expect something back even if they say they will not. By sending you something they find something out about you, such as your mobile phone number or address.
- **Never give out your parent's credit card information**.

beSmart beSafe

- **Tell your parents or a trusted adult** if someone is communicating with you on the internet and it does not feel 'right'.
- **Beware of sharing secrets** with online friends that can be used to blackmail you later.

- **Have an agreement with your parents on the sites you can visit that cost money**.
- **Separate your friends between your physical world and your virtual world**: real friends and cyberpals. Do this in your IM. In this way you ban be sure not to make mistakes when switching between conversations.
- **Never give out your password to anyone**, even your best friend.
- **Ask your parents to help find child-friendly blog space**: here can you post and share information with your trusted friends.
- **Do not click attachments to emails** unless you are sure you know who they are from.
- **Ask your parents to install software that blocks sites** that you do not feel comfortable visiting. This could be sites containing sex or violence.

Take a journey

You know it can be difficult even for those technical savvy parents amongst us to really appreciate our children's excitement when they go online, particularly when their online activities threaten to encroach on other more healthy activities, such as football and running around outside, the sort of stuff that we did when we were kids, and then of course there is their school work. You will observe when they walk through the door as they beeline for the computer how absorbed they are and how they become completely disconnected from the real world.

So what is the cure to this madness? Well it is time you took a journey with your children online. Read the section on gaming first and then see what they like to do and where they like to go and 'hang out'. Be ready to be surprised. Hold back on negative observations: do not judge and let the positive and inquisitive part of you take over. Then let your children rule the moment.

Ask them to show you their favourite online forums, chatrooms and sites. Get to know your children's online friends and correspondents. It will help you to begin to understand how to help balance your values and your children's preferences. Learn to see the world through their eyes. With this trust your children should not be afraid to tell you anything. Encourage your children to come to you when they are uncomfortable. Make yourself worthy of their trust by understanding.

With this insight you should then have the required knowledge to better negotiate with your children about the priorities in their lives with less conflict than before. Together you can start to develop a set of rules to govern the online behaviour of you both. The high-level rules are simple:

1. ensure that your children are safe;
2. improve your ability to become more experienced on your children's net activities; and
3. thus gain the approval of your children in their online world.

CYBERBULLYING AND MOBBING

Cyberbullying is the virtual form of bullying and mobbing and normally includes sending or posting of harmful or cruel text or images using the internet or other digital communication devices. Incidences of cyberbullying can occur in chatrooms, via IM or SMS/MMS (Multimedia Messaging Service). The Anti-Bullying Alliance recently found that one in five schoolchildren in the UK had been the victim of some form of online or mobile abuse. Many incidences of bullying through malicious SMS messages have been reported in schools. There have been several well-publicised teenage suicides as a result of cyberbullying. It is more intrusive than physical bullying because it is invasive, it follows the child everywhere and there is no escape. Some countries are running advertising campaigns to shed some light on this problem as it is extremely difficult for any child to know how to best deal with this, particularly given the potential scale of cyberbullying. For example you can have 60 people bullying you on the internet, but in real life there would not be 60 people beating you up. Cyberbullying takes many forms and some examples of cyberbullying could include the following (see http://www.direct.gov.uk/en/YoungPeople/HealthAndRelationships/Bullying/DG_070501).

- **Email**: sending emails that can be threatening or upsetting. Emails can be sent directly to a single target or to a group of people to encourage them to become part of the bullying. These messages or 'hate mail' can include examples of racism, sexism and other types of prejudice.
- **IM and chatrooms**: sending IM and chatroom messages to friends or directly to a victim. Others can be invited into the bullying conversation.
- **Social networking sites**: setting up profiles on social networking sites to make fun of someone. By visiting these pages or contributing to them, you become part of the problem and add to the feelings of unhappiness felt by the victim.
- **Mobile phone**: sending humiliating and abusive text or video messages, as well as photo messages and phone calls over a mobile phone. This includes anonymous text messages over short distances using Bluetooth technology and sharing videos of physical attacks on individuals (happy slapping) or taking a picture of a person in the changing room using a digital phone camera and sending that picture to others.
- **Interactive gaming**: games consoles allow players to chat online with anyone they find themselves matched with in a multiplayer game. Sometimes cyberbullies abuse other players and use threats. They can also lock victims out of games, spread false rumours about someone or hack into someone's account.
- **Sending viruses**: some people send viruses or hacking programs to another person that can destroy their computers or delete personal information from their hard drive.
- **Abusing personal information**: many victims of cyberbullying have complained that they have seen personal

photos, emails or blog postings posted where others could see them without their permission. Social networking sites make it a lot easier for web users to get hold of personal information and photos of people. They can also get hold of someone else's messaging accounts and chat to people pretending to be the victim.

Ryan Patrick Halligan is well-publicised example in the United States of a teenager that took his own life following a long spate of cyberbullying. Ryan's parents realised when he was very young that his speech, language and motor skills development were not at the same level as their other children at the same age. Ryan received special education from pre-school through to the fourth grade. However as he became older he became aware that he was not as academically strong as most of his classmates.

> 'Now certainly my son was not the first boy in history to be bullied . . . But when I discovered a folder filled with IM exchanges throughout the summer and further interviewed his classmates, I realized that technology was being utilized as weapons far more effective and reaching then the simple ones we had as kids. Passing handwritten notes or a "slam" book[3] has since been replaced with on-line tools such as IM, Websites, Blogs, cell phones, etc. The list keeps growing with the invention of every new hi-tech communication gadget . . . I believe my son would have survived these incidents of bullying and humiliation if they took place before computers and the internet . . . I believe bullying through technology has the effect of accelerating and amplifying the hurt to new levels . . .'
>
> JOHN HALLIGAN, the father of Ryan Patrick Halligan,
> http://www.ryanpatrickhalligan.org

Ryan's father found out the reason for his son's suicide because the last rule on his list of online rules was 'no secret passwords'. The other rules resembled those provided in the previous section, but his last rule was a safety rule just in case any of his children did not follow the preceding rules. With the password he could have instant access to all of their online activities. This rule ended up revealing the truth behind the mystery of why his son took his own life.

Some good advice on how to deal with cyberbullying is:

- talk to someone you trust about it, such as a friend, a teacher or an older relative;
- keep and save any bullying emails, text messages or images you receive;
- make a note of the time and date that messages or images were sent, along with any details you have about the sender;
- try changing your online user ID or nickname;
- change your mobile phone number and only give it out to close friends;
- mobile phone companies and internet service providers can trace bullies, so do not be afraid of reporting it to them;
- block IMs from certain people or use mail filters to block emails from specific email addresses;
- do not reply to bullying or threatening text messages or emails as this could make matters worse and lets those carrying out the bullying know that they have found a 'live' phone number or email address;
- report serious bullying, such as threats of a physical or sexual nature, to the police.

The Directgov website at http://yp.direct.gov.uk/cyberbullying/ provides further information about cyberbullying.

GAMING AND VIRTUAL WORLDS

Interactive gaming is a large and addictive play world. Participants can become so immersed in the game that the physical world that they live in can become an extension of their virtual world.

For those of us that have never been enticed into the gaming world it is difficult to understand the attraction that gaming has, particularly when we hear stories on the addictive nature of gaming. It starts with gaming on the PC, which is quite safe for your children, if not a little addictive. Later on they will migrate to the online gaming world and here there are risks to their privacy and ultimately to their safety. There is more on this in the next chapter.

Those games that have gained significant publicity are those within virtual worlds where they will meet other gamers and build their online reputations based on their performance and ability to meet common goals. They will make online friends that they meet regularly virtually to play together and support each other, or compete against each other, in a structured gaming world whereby they have become a part of the gaming infrastructure.

This section takes just a few examples and we start with a 'game' that is not really considered as a computer game, but more of a global community that uses the internet and some high-tech gadgets. Then we take a look at a couple of games that can be also useful as learning aids: The Sims and Sid Meier's Civilization. Finally we take a look at World of Warcraft (WoW) to better understand what all of the hype is about.

Not all of these games pose a threat to you or your children's identity or privacy, they are just fun. It is a great way to get linked up with your children; it puts you on the same wavelength. The idea is that your children will not hesitate to ask for your help when they are online and something happens that they feel uncomfortable about, because they will understand that you just 'get it'.

The high tech Easter egg hunt

'It's a high tech Easter egg hunt. The player hides a container of inexpensive articles – referred to as cache. Then they post its latitude & longitude on the internet
(Continued)

(Continued)

(http://www.geocaching.com/), and then other players go hunting for it. If they find it they trade the contents and sign a log to record their visit. The minimum you have to have to play is a computer connected to the internet and a handheld GPSr (Global Positioning Satellite receiver).'

Getting started with Geocaching,
http://www.geocaching.com/about/

The game is called Geocaching (Figure 4.1). Participants use a GPS receiver or other navigational techniques to hide and seek containers (called 'geocaches' or 'caches') anywhere in the world. A typical cache is a small waterproof container containing a logbook and 'treasure', usually toys or trinkets of little value. Today well over 480,000 geocaches are registered on various websites devoted to the sport. Geocaches are currently placed in over 100 countries around the world and on all seven continents including Antarctica.

FIGURE 4.1   *Geocaching*
(reproduced by permission
of Birgitta Karnfält)

There are different variants of geocache. For the traditional geocache, a geocacher will place a waterproof container, containing a logbook (with pen or pencil) and trinkets or some sort of treasure and then note the cache's coordinates. These coordinates, along with other details of the location, are posted on the geocachers' website. Other geocachers obtain the coordinates from the internet and seek out the cache using their GPS handheld receivers. The geocachers that find the cache record their exploits first in the logbook and then online. Geocachers are free to take objects from the cache in exchange for leaving something of similar or higher value, so there is treasure for the next person to find. Some geocaches requires one to discover information in order to find the cache; this could involve solving a puzzle in order to determine the final cache location.

Typical cache treasures are not high in monetary value but may hold personal value to the finder. Aside from the logbook, common cache contents are unusual coins or currency, small toys, ornamental buttons, CDs or books. Also common are objects that are moved from cache to cache, such as Travel Bugs or Geocoins, whose travels may be logged and followed online. Occasionally higher value items are included in geo-caches, normally reserved for the 'first finder' or in locations which are harder to reach.

If a geocache has been vandalised or stolen it is said to have been 'muggled' or 'plundered'. The former term plays off the fact that those not familiar with geocaching are called 'geo-muggles' or just 'muggles', a term borrowed from the Harry Potter books. If a cacher discovers that a cache has been muggled, it can be logged as needing maintenance, which sends an email to the cache owner so that it can be repaired, replaced or archived (deactivated).

The real fun is discovering endless new parks and interesting places near you that you never knew were there. It is absolutely astounding how many interesting places there are near you that you are probably unaware of. Drag your children away from the computer for this high-tech Easter egg hunt and bring them back to the real world. They will love it and you will love it, as it provides the setting for outdoor family fun.

The Sims

Gaming demographics are predominately male. However it is The Sims that has effectively broken this trend. Daughters will be enchanted by The Sims and you will be fascinated to see how the dollhouses of our generation have become digitised. This game is perfectly safe for your young children to play as it is stored locally on the computer and has no online interaction.

The Sims is one of a number of games that are structured as a 'series'. These types of games have no specific end goal, so they never stop. Many of these are called 'life simulations'. In The Sims this involves creating a persona, this could be a boy, girl, animal or person. The player chooses how their persona will look and how they will act. Making the persona happy is achieved by balancing a number of energy bars labelled bladder, hunger, energy, comfort, hygiene, social, fun and room. In fact using this game children can experiment and learn.

For example what happens when their persona has all work and no play? They can try to match The Sims life to match their own and see what happens when they change certain parameters. You as the parent could have some fun joining your children's digital dollhouse and performing some experiments.

Sid Meier's Civilization

Another game that is installed locally and has no online interaction with other players is Sid Meier's Civilization. This game has been around for years and even right back to the very early versions the game was very successful in covering the whole scope of human endeavour encompassing history, philosophy, science, art and basically everything that makes things in civilizations work or fail.

This game will appeal to teenagers and poses no threat to the privacy of the player. The player will create, live and breathe in their virtual world where they are tasked the role as head of an entire empire. In this role they need to conquer the world against the computer, which plays the opposition. Players can choose from over 20 different civilisations from the Aztecs and Babylonians to the Celts, Greeks, Romans, Vikings and Zulus. During the course of the game there is much to discover including political philosophies, such as monarchy and feudalism, early discoveries, such as the alphabet and the wheel, and technologies that have shaped the world as we know it today: medicine, electricity, flight, nuclear power and genetic engineering.

The game starts with the player in control of a small colony that expands and prospers as the player gains proficiency. The player learns for example what happens to their colony when they choose to spend money on expanding the empire (equipping the army) as opposed to growing essentials such as rice needed for the survival of the colony.

Civilization starts with a beguiling simplicity that quickly grows to become so large and complex that it is not only overwhelming but incredibly addictive in its nature. Enjoy the long conversations that you will have with your children as they try to balance the elements within their colony: they want to grow their colony and so they build their army ready for war, only to be driven back to basics by famine because of the lack of investment in life basics. You may enjoy the role of trusted advisor in their online fantasy world.

In fact it is a fascinating game for children and it can feel quite nice for parents to know that their children learn about how things work in the real world and that they learn in a way that they would never learn at school.

World of Warcraft

WoW is played by over four million people worldwide. It is one of the online virtual worlds that are called massively multiplayer online role playing games (MMORPGs). It is all about dungeons, dragons, swords and sorcery. WoW differentiates itself among other similar games in that you are playing with thousands of other people. Every character in WoW has a real person behind it, all online in the same universe at the same time. In these types of online world players do not use their own names, so this enables you to keep your online epics separate from your physical or real life, although the gaming company knows who you are because you need to pay a subscription with your credit card.

Apart from the obvious online gaming addiction problem associated with WoW there is also a risk that your children may accept gifts online. These may not necessarily be perceived as gifts given their virtual nature, but they are. These gifts can take the form of charms that the player needs in order to advance to the next level or new shiny armour for example. In the previous chapter we outlined how this may be used during the online grooming process.

Mentoring is a part of the game. Mentoring, although in principal a good practice, if abused can be used as part of the 'grooming' of children in WoW.

> 'We met in the WoW, doing a quest in a party with some other people. The way we cooperated did click and we did quests together often. My character was about 10–15 levels higher than that of hers. So I could easily protect that character and gain easy experience points to level her character.'
>
> ANONYMOUS, February 2008

WoW is staged as a game of epic conflict between the two factions of Horde (evil) and Alliance (good). For example the Alliance contains collections of humans, night elves, dwarves and gnomes, with hearts of gold and appearances to match. The Horde is the evil side: Orcs, Tauren, Undead and Trolls.

The Horde races are considerably less attractive than their rivals and look intimidating.

This is just the start of a journey into a fantasy world. The game draws you in, as does the prospect of taking this journey with other people sitting behind each of these characters that could be living anywhere in the world. It is the community feeling within WoW that makes it so attractive. It is like an enormous chatroom where everyone has something in common: that burning desire for in-game success, fame and fortune. On the battleground, friendships are formed and real-life rivalries developed.

The game is absorbing and compulsive in its nature, meaning that pulling your children away from the computer may be bad for your health. Not pulling them away occasionally for a break will most certainly be bad for their health. Then of course what happens if it is you that gets lost in this virtual world? There is no cure. You need to find a system that works for you and your family if you or your charges are to find yourself one day in WoW.

Second Life

Neal Stephenson's 1992 novel *Snow Crash* envisioned a futuristic virtual world called the metaverse in which characters controlled digital representations of themselves (known as avatars) in a shared online environment. Today instead of one cohesive metaverse there are hundreds of virtual worlds in existence with themes ranging from fantasy to science fiction to idealised modern environments.

Second Life was initially conceived as an empty virtual world with a population of 3.3 million virtual people (avatars) in 2007, each with real physical identities behind each one of them. Every avatar has an alias name. Gartner have predicted that, by the end of 2011, 80 per cent of active internet users will have some sort of presence in a virtual world, with Second Life currently one of the most populous.

The social side of Second Life attracts many players. Residents in Second Life can buy their own island, create their dream house, become a clothing designer, go fishing, spend nights partying in clubs and bars and, of course, have virtual sex with virtual people. There is also a teen variant of Second Life and of course there is no sex here. However there is nothing to stop a minor from installing the full Second Life program and creating an avatar, they just need to lie about their age. The risks to privacy in Second Life are that everything you do here is digitally stored in one of their databases that have the potential to be mined. Although you can live in Second Life for free, to have any fun you need to pay something and for this you need a credit card. So your avatar is linked to your credit card. This means that everything that you do in Second Life can be linked to your real identity, including virtual sex. Second Life is based in the United States so this data can be sold to the highest bidder.

Everything in Second Life costs Linden Dollars (L$) which can be purchased using real money. It is possible to exchange real money to L$ and back again using the L$ exchange rate. Second Life is probably the only self-sustained economy on the internet in that Second Life provides its residents with the equivalent of atoms, small elements of virtual matter called 'primitives', so that they can build things from scratch. Thanks to these property rights, residents actively trade their creations. Of about 10 million objects created, about 230,000 are bought and sold every month in the in-world currency L$. This devotion to what is termed as 'user-generated content' now places it at the centre of the Web 2.0 trend.

The real beauty of Second Life is that you are unrestricted by those physical, cultural and social boundaries of your physical environment. You create an avatar and evolve your virtual identity. Over time this could include the purchase of additional avatar abilities or commodities that facilitate the evolution of your online experience and reputation. In Second Life you meet other residents and become part of Second Life communities, just like in the real world.

Gaming addiction

Computer games can be magical, fantasy driven or violent while others simulate real life. Online games such as WoW involve real people that are the driving force behind fantasy characters. These games are exciting and addictive and for some people their gaming life can take over their real lives. This is a known problem and for those families that know they have a household member that has lost the thin line between reality and fantasy it may be time to get some help, particularly if it is affecting their school grades, their performance at work or relations within the family. People that game obsessively stop caring about the physical world; what they see as real is the online fantasy world, so it is difficult to bring them crashing back to reality.

There have been three well-documented deaths caused directly by exhaustion from playing games for long periods (NationMaster.com 2008a). In South Korea, Lee Seung Seop (NationMaster.com 2008b) died after playing Starcraft for over 50 hours. In Jinzhou, China, Xu Yan died after playing online games for over 15 days during the Lunar New Year holiday and an unnamed 30-year-old died in Guangzhou, China after playing for 3 days straight.

There are support groups available to help with this. To understand more about the problem and how it is being researched the Center for Internet Addiction Recovery (http://www.netaddiction.com/) provides support as does On-line Gamers Anonymous (http://www.olganonboard.org/), which is an online resource that provides a 12-step self-help process dedicated to helping those addicted to online games.

5 All in the Name of National Safety

In recent years governments throughout the world have enacted legislation intended to comprehensively increase their reach into the private life of every living person. Hence it does not matter where we live, what we do or who we are; this has an impact on every one of us. This has all been done in the name of national security, encompassing law enforcement, the fight against terrorism and illegal immigration, administrative efficiency and welfare fraud. This legislation has effectively rendered the fundamental right of privacy fragile and exposed. Fear has taken on a new form: it is shapeless, and no longer tangible. Tangible fear is generated from first-hand experiences. Media and governments feed on our fear, a misplaced fear; after all it is fear that we have been spoon fed from the media.

The extent of surveillance over the lives of many people has reached an unprecedented level. This is 'security theatre' in its prime. Security theatre consists of security controls that are implemented just to make us feel safer, whether they are effective or not is irrelevant. A perfect example of security theatre is the life vests under our seats when we fly and the charade we (and the cabin attendants) need to endure before take-off. We can wonder why they do not place parachutes under our seats, after all would they not offer a much more effective safety measure than a life vest?

Then we have the laws that protect privacy and freedoms that are frequently flawed and riddled with exceptions. At the same time technological advances, technology standards, interoperability between information systems and the globalisation of information have placed extraordinary pressure on the few remaining privacy safeguards. The effect of these developments has been to create surveillance societies that nurture hostile environments for privacy.

Each year since 1997, the US-based Electronic Privacy Information Center and the UK-based Privacy International have undertaken what has now become the most comprehensive survey of global privacy ever published. The *Privacy and Human Rights Report* (Privacy International 2007a) surveys developments in more than 75 countries, assessing the state of surveillance and privacy protection.

In this chapter we give a taste of some of the challenges that face these countries and some insight into the justification behind their rating awarded by Privacy International. The total report runs over more than 1,100 pages.

A RIGHT TO PRIVACY

'Privacy is a fundamental human right. It underpins human dignity and other values such as freedom of association and freedom of speech. It has become one of the most important human rights of the modern age.'

PRIVACY INTERNATIONAL, 2008a

Privacy is recognised around the world in diverse regions and cultures. It is protected in the *Universal Declaration of Human Rights* (United Nations 1948), the *International Covenant on Civil and Political Rights* (United Nations 1966) and in many other international and regional human rights treaties. Nearly every country in the world includes a right of privacy in its constitution. Surprisingly some countries that do not are the UK and the United States. However the right for privacy although not explicitly defined in the constitution is implicitly acknowledged as a right.

In addition in those countries where privacy is not explicitly recognised in the constitution, the courts have found that right in other provisions. In many countries international agreements that recognise privacy rights such as the *International*

Covenant on Civil and Political Rights or the *European Convention on Human Rights* (Council of Europe 1950) have been adopted into law.

According to Privacy International (2008b) privacy can be divided into the following distinct but related concepts.

- **Information privacy**, which involves the establishment of rules governing the collection and handling of personal data such as credit information and medical and government records. It is also known as 'data protection'.
- **Bodily privacy**, which concerns the protection of people's physical selves against invasive procedures such as genetic tests, drug testing and cavity searches.
- **Privacy of communications**, which covers the security and privacy of mail, telephone calls, email and other forms of communication.
- **Territorial privacy**, which concerns the setting of limits on intrusion into the domestic and other environments such as the workplace or public space. This includes searches, video surveillance and ID checks.

INFORMATION PRIVACY

Constitutional privacy framework and legislation

A constitution is a system for governance, often codified as a written document that establishes the rules and principles of an autonomous political entity. In the case of countries the constitution defines the fundamental political principles, established structure, procedures, powers and duties of a government. Most national constitutions also guarantee certain rights to the people, such as the basic right for privacy, although some do not. For example the UK does not have a written constitution on a subject's right to privacy although the *Human Rights Act* provides for a limited incorporation of the *European Convention on Human Rights* into domestic law, including the right for privacy. The United States has no right to privacy in its constitution although search and seizure protections exist in the *4th Amendment*.

In order to be able to enforce a constitution a legal framework needs to be in place so that the written constitution can be enforced. These laws should protect the right to privacy against governments and companies, should include sectoral laws, e.g. medical privacy, workplace privacy and financial privacy, and they should be effective.

In addition to the absence of a privacy constitutional framework the United States also lacks an extensive privacy law; its approach to data privacy has a strong cultural bias and a business philosophy for self-regulation with minimal federal legislation and some state legislation. Examples of some federal legislation include the *Health Insurance Portability and Accountability Act* (HIPAA) (US Department of Health and Human Services 1996) which has had a far reaching impact on the American healthcare sector enforcing the protection of patients' medical records, the *Gramm– Leach–Bliley Act* (US Senate Committee on Banking, Housing, and Urban Affairs 1999) which protects the privacy of an individual's financial records and the *Children's Online Privacy Protection Act* (Federal Trade Commission 1998) which was enacted to add controls on the collection of personal information on children.

The European Union

Did you know that the *UK Data Protection Act* (DPA) empowers you as the data subject with the right to know what is stored on you and by whom? The DPA includes the right for transparency. This means that you as a British citizen have the right to know what is stored about you, whether this is by government authorities or other organisations holding personal information that can be linked directly back to your identity. All you need to do is make a formal request to the data holding authority and as long as the parameters of your request are reasonable they have no choice but to fulfil it.

In 1995 the European Union enacted the *EU Directive on Data Privacy (95/46/EC)* (European Commission 1995) in order to harmonise member states' laws in providing consistent levels of protection for citizens and ensuring the free flow of personal data within the European Union. The directive sets a baseline common level of privacy that not only reinforces current data protection law, but also establishes a range of new rights. A key concept in the European data protection model is 'enforceability'. Data subjects have rights established in explicit rules. Every European Union country has a data protection commissioner or agency that enforces the rules. It is expected that the countries with which Europe does business will need to provide a similar level of oversight.

Hence in Europe information privacy is a basic human right supported by the *EU Directive on Data Privacy (95/46/EC)*. Every member state should have a privacy protection law in place to enforce this directive. For example in the UK there is the *Data Protection Act 1998* (Information Commissioner's Office 1998). UK organisations that collect personal data must register with the government and take precautions against the misuse of data. The act prohibits the collection, use and dissemination of personal information without the individual's consent. The individual has the right to know what their data is being collected for and that their personal information is not being sold or used for other purposes. Organisations are obliged to tell individuals the reasons for information collection, to provide access to the information stored and correct any inaccurate data that may have been stored on that individual. Finally these organisations must demonstrate that personal information is kept secure and inaccessible to unauthorised parties. An example of what this means to you if you live in the UK is that your medical records cannot be shared with any party without your permission, that you have the right to access this information and that your health authority has an obligation to ensure that your private data is stored securely. The act also protects you against companies that have personal information on you from selling this to countries that are not adhering to the same rules as are regulated

113

in the EU. Take a look at the section on the 'The Safe Harbor Agreement' for more information on sharing of personal information between the EU and the United States.

Asia-Pacific Economic Cooperation

'The *APEC Privacy Framework* promotes a flexible approach to information privacy protection for APEC Member Economies, while avoiding the creation of unnecessary barriers to information flows.'

APEC, 2005

APEC (Asia-Pacific Economic Cooperation) began as an informal ministerial-level dialogue group with 12 members in 1989. By 2003 APEC had grown to 21 economies when they commenced development of an Asia-Pacific privacy standard. The idea of the standard was to provide 'a practical policy approach to enable accountability in the flow of data while preventing impediments to trade'. It provides technical assistance to those APEC economies that have not addressed privacy from a regulatory or policy perspective. The nine principles of the *APEC Privacy Framework* are (APEC 2005):

- preventing harm;
- integrity of personal information;
- notice;
- security safeguards;
- collection limitations;
- access and correction;
- uses of personal information;
- accountability;
- choice.

A Privacy Sub Group was set up comprising Australia, Canada, China, Hong Kong, Japan, Korea, Malaysia, New Zealand, Thailand and the United States to manage this. In March 2004 Version 9 of the *APEC Privacy Principles* was released as a public consultation draft. APEC Ministers endorsed the *APEC*

Privacy Framework in November 2004. In 2005 APEC reported that they were on track in the creation of the *APEC Privacy Framework*. Progress on the *APEC Privacy Framework* can be found on the Privacy International website where they have a report on the Asia-Pacific privacy process (Privacy International 2008c).

Iberoamerican data protection

In 2007 a seminar was held in Columbia with representatives of 12 Latin American countries in addition to Spain and Portugal. At this seminar the need to implement harmonised measures for the protection of personal data was stressed that would enable the free flow of information, thus facilitating trade. Just as with the United States, different data protection levels in Latin American and Europe represent an obstacle to the flow of information that in turn is hindering economic activities. It is a significant problem because very few Latin American countries have privacy legislation in this area.

The Safe Harbor Agreement

As the US approach to information privacy is mainly self-regulated with minimal federal legislation and some state legislation, it is in no way as encompassing or far reaching as the *EU Data Protection Directive* in how your personal data must be protected. Although some members of Congress in the United States have tried to pass proprivacy legislation, they have been blocked. There is a group called NetCoalition.com, with members including AOL, amazon.com, Yahoo!, eBay and DoubleClick that lobby for self-regulation.

The European Commission had never issued a formal opinion on the adequacy of privacy protection in the United States; they have nonetheless serious doubts whether the US sectoral and self-regulatory approach to privacy protection would pass the adequacy standard set out in the EU Directive. Hence the idea of the *Safe Harbor* was instigated permitting US companies the option to voluntarily self-certify to adhere to a set of privacy principles worked out by the US Department of Commerce and the Internal Market Directorate of the European Commission. The Commission approved the *Safe Habor Agreement* on 26 July 2000. All participating companies are presumed to adhere to those privacy principles as set out by the agreement which means that they could continue to receive personal data from the European Union.

The principles require all signatory organisations to provide individuals with 'clear and conspicuous' notice of the kind of information they collect, the purposes for which it may be used and any third parties to whom it may be disclosed. This notice must be given at the time of the collection of any personal information or 'as soon thereafter as is practicable'. Individuals must be given the ability to choose (opt-out of) the collection of data where the information is either going to be disclosed to a third party or used for an incompatible purpose. In the case of sensitive information individuals must expressly consent (opt-in) to the collection. Organisations wishing to transfer data to a third party may do so if the third party subscribes to the *Safe Harbor Agreement* or if that third party signs an agreement to protect the data (Export Gov 2008).

- These organisations must take reasonable precautions to protect the security of information against loss, misuse and unauthorised access, disclosure, alteration and destruction.
- Organisations must provide individuals with access to any personal information held about them and individuals must be provided with the opportunity to correct, amend or delete that information where it is inaccurate. This right is to be granted only if the burden or expense of providing access would not be disproportionate to the risks to the individual's privacy or where the rights of persons other than the individual would not be violated.
- When it comes to enforcement organisations must provide access to readily available and affordable

independent recourse mechanisms that may investigate complaints and award damages. They must issue follow-up compliance procedures and must adhere to sanctions for failing to comply with the principles.

Types of data collected

Our willingness to share personal data has evolved: we have for years been sharing our personal and often sensitive data with government authorities and normally we do not have much choice in this. In the name of national safety the government is busy collecting information on us in new and increasingly ingenious ways; furthermore companies use data gathered from us in order to make money. For them privacy is bad for business.

Key types of data that can be collected are personally identifiable information (PII), sensitive data, aggregate data and anonymous data.

Personally identifiable information

All personal information collected on us that can be linked directly to our identity is PII. PII is behaviour that can be linked directly or indirectly to you. PII can include sensitive data if it is linked to your identity. It is your PII that you leave behind in your everyday life that forms your digital footprints. All information collected on you by government authorities is PII; any information collected on you with the use of store cards is PII; any information collected via the use of cookies on your PC when you shop is PII. A new development in early 2008 was that a committee of European Union data privacy commissioners determined that IP addresses (the numerical codes that identify a computer when it connects to the internet) are personal information. Defining IP addresses as PII means big changes are in store for some companies, such as search engine operators which capture and store IP addresses. Google maintains its position that IP addresses are not associated with individual users, but merely with the location of a particular computer.

Did you know that everything that you do online and offline, if digitally stored somewhere and linked to your PII, becomes a part of your virtual shadow? Your virtual shadow is the accumulation of digital footprints that you leave behind.

Sensitive data

Sensitive data as defined by the *EU Data Protection Directive* is data that is revealing of racial or ethnic origin, political opinions, religious or philosophical beliefs, trade-union membership and data concerning health or sex life. Your health records are sensitive data as is your DNA.

Aggregate and anonymous data

Aggregate data is information that is grouped for analysis, typically stated in percentages. An example is that 87 per cent of children use the computer regularly in Sweden. Anonymous data is information that is not personally identifiable because it is not linked directly or indirectly with any unique individual and it could be that it has been stripped of unique identifiers. This can be data that has had the PII stripped to convert it into aggregate data.

How anonymous the data really is after stripping PII is open to discussion. For example in July 2008 the House of Lords overruled the Scottish Information Commissioner's decision to allow the release of anonymised regional medical statistics, saying that the data was still private and thus covered under the UK's *Data Protection Act*. The controversy stems from a request by a Scottish parliamentary researcher for leukaemia data related to children in the 0–14 years of age group from a specific postal region. The Lords' ruling was based on the low rate of incidents, which could have made it possible to correlate the data with individuals in spite of the fact that the data had been anonymised (OUT-LAW.com 2008).

Sharing of medical and other sensitive information

Most of us feel pretty strongly concerning keeping our medical records private for good reasons, it is our 'sensitive data'. Owing to the sensitivity of the data most countries do have laws in place to either treat medical data as sensitive or protect health privacy rights.

How our medical data is being managed has undergone a dramatic transition over the last 10–15 years with the migration of medical data originally stored in paper format onto digital media. The main risk to our medical data when it was stored in filing cabinets was that the wrong person had access, although this had to be physical access. Another risk was when medical data had to be sent to another health authority which happens when you move house for example.

Now the challenge that the medical profession has is that although your medical data is digitised it is nonetheless still sitting in one place. So if you move or if you are on vacation or away on business in another part of the country, there is still a process needed to send your medical data from health authority A to health authority B. Hence a vision that several governments around the world are looking to execute is the linking of medical data. There has been a lot of publicity in the UK on the privacy concerns. Dr Ross Anderson a professor of security engineering has worked extensively on the project and has also published numerous papers on the perils of centralising patient data. Nevertheless many countries are taking this route. An example of what this means in practice is shown in Figure 5.1.

Australia is today linking electronic health records between health authorities and the UK is planning to move in this direction. It is normal that the authorised personnel are first authenticated by the identity management system (i.e. where the linked medical data is stored).

There are three systems holding health records: (1) health authority A, (2) health authority B and (3) a central database

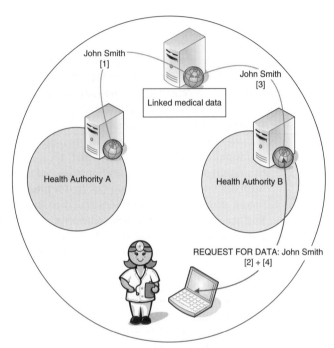

FIGURE 5.1   *Linking health records*

where key health records for both health authorities A and B are stored (linked medical data).

1. Health authorities A and B have synchronised all key patient health records to the linked medical data database. This could be just the patient ID and key data such as address and which health authority they belong to.

2. After authentication a doctor makes a request for data on John Smith who is has just moved from health authority A to health authority B.

3. John Smith's details have already been copied (synchronised) into the database at health authority B on notification of his move.

4. If the doctor is authorised they receive access to the requested data.

This is just one variation of several types of possible architectures for 'identity management'. Another variation is by using the principle of 'trust' (this uses a concept called 'federation' as the underlying architectural principle) between health authorities. The ability for an identity management system to provide single sign-on (which eliminates the need for an authorised person to remember different passwords for each system that they authenticate to, i.e. are given access to) means that an authorised party is automatically authenticated to additional systems. What is important and common for all is that key patient data is stored in one national repository that can be accessed by any person that has the required authorisation irrelevant of where they are physically. The most pressing concerns are as follows.

- First the sensitivity of this data makes it even more vulnerable if there is just one data breach. Imagine if all patient records where in one place: this would make it an even more attractive target for potential hackers; small hacks become big hacks worth more money. We list some examples.
  - ✦ It was recorded by the data privacy authority in 2007 that France had many security breaches identified in computerised patient records.
  - ✦ The Norwegian government merged a number of welfare databases without implementing adequate access restrictions.
  - ✦ In Sweden medical records are linked and regulated by sector specific law, but there are inadequate policies implemented to protect access to data.
  - ✦ In the United States there is only weak protection for medical privacy. Potentially the FBI biometric database could prove to be the largest database of biometrics around the world that is not protected by strong privacy law.
- Second is that once centralised how long will it take before some national emergency surfaces that necessitates the need to use this data in a way that is a direct infringement on our personal privacy? In other words

mission or function creep occurs (i.e. the expansion of a project or mission beyond its original goals, such as DNA collected for research later being used to solve crimes).

The linking of medical records in an identity management system enables the medical files to be linked to a national unique ID card and this practice is gathering some interest in certain countries. This means that your medical records can be accessed directly from your ID card as is the case today in Sweden. This has many advantages, mainly that you should receive the correct treatment in the event of an emergency as your unique identifier will be linked to your medical records. It is generally accepted in Sweden that the linking of medical records is a good thing; benefits include improved healthcare services and peace of mind that the availability of records improves the quality of the treatment received by patients. The attending doctor can see immediately if you have a medical condition that could influence how they should treat you. In the United States they have taken this a step further whereby some hospitals offer patients with special health conditions such as epilepsy, diabetes and Alzheimer's disease a radio-frequency identification (RFID) implant.

Do you want your sensitive data on your ID card?

Belgium issues smart ID cards from the age of six: the card may contain data such as medical files for use in public and private sectors. Finland's new identity card includes voluntary medical insurance data. Poland has a new law that requires a national identifier to be used for filling prescriptions. Switzerland has plans to store medical information on new health insurance cards. In Taiwan patient ID cards include a smartcard solution with illnesses encoded on the card

Google opened a new online filing cabinet service for medical applications on 19 May 2008 called 'Google Health'

(Tribune Wire 2008). The service permits users to have a single online repository for all facets of their medical history including records, X-rays and information about allergies, vaccinations and prescriptions. Google is partnering with healthcare providers so that if the user chooses, a doctor, nurse, pharmacy or insurance company can also upload records and other information and access the profile. Users would enter certain information about themselves like allergies, age and personal characteristics, while other items such as X-rays, test results and immunisation records would be added to the profile by an authorised healthcare provider, such as a doctor's office or hospital.

Google is not the first to come up with this concept; Microsoft has already introduced a similar product called HealthVault (Microsoft 2008). Announced partners on Google Health include Walgreens, Quest Diagnostics, the American Medical Association, the American Heart Association, several large hospitals and several providers of personal health records. Google plans to announce more partnerships in the coming weeks. Apparently Google Health will not be subject to HIPAA which governs the privacy of medical records in the United States.

All in the name of child safety

'Increasing amounts of information about children are being collected and shared between agencies, including assessments that purport to show whether a child is "at risk" of becoming a criminal. Several systems already exist to hold this data and information about the "diversionary" schemes on which the child has been placed. This whole policy is extremely controversial, and many leading academics disagree that likely criminality can be predicted from data such as family income and housing, or even from low-level delinquency.'

ACTION RIGHTS FOR CHILDREN (ARCH),
http://www.arch-ed.org/

The emergence of an information society has its costs and one of them is that we are collecting increasing amounts of personal information on our children. Each country has its own approach. In Austria they have been storing all data on their children for the last 60 years and this data is centralised in one database. In Belgium they issue smart ID cards to children from the age of six that can include data such as medical files for use in both public and private sectors.

In 2008 the Netherlands and Australia have both been busy. The Netherlands plans to implement a database of all children to record development from birth, similar to what is going on in the UK today (the Children's Index). Australia has started registration for the Access card. Along with the introduction of the Access card a centralised, national population data-base called the Access Card Register will be implemented. This database will also hold details of children as well as adults, but only adults will be issued with a card. The data-base will include biometric photographs.

The UK has been busy too, all in the name of child safety: children personal data is being collected and stored in data-bases that are or will be merged. This is commonly referred to as the Children's Index, but in fact it is much more than this.

Every child matters

Prevention rather than cure has its obvious attractions. The UK government has started initiatives to help identify cases of child abuse earlier and also to tackle disadvantages facing children and young people. Both of these initiatives involve collecting personal information on children and storing that data in a central database that can be mined.

'Every Child Matters: Change for Children' (http://www.everychildmatters.gov.uk/aims/) is a new approach to the well-being of children and young people from birth to age 19 that was triggered by the abuse and eventual death of Victoria Climbié by her guardians. In this case the abuse of Victoria slipped through the social services net and she died at the hands of her abusive guardians.

The government hopes that sharing information on children will improve child welfare in the UK and reduce the incidence of serious child abuse such as in the Climbié case. However a report prepared by the Foundation for Information Policy Research (Anderson et al. 2006) points out that extending Britain's child protection systems from the 50,000 children at substantial risk of serious harm to the 3 to 4 million children with some health, education or other welfare issue means that those children who are most at risk may in fact receive less attention. They also conclude that the systems will intrude so much into privacy and family life that they will violate data protection law and human rights law.

'The association of "Every Child Matters" with Victoria Climbie and the repeated use of expressions such as "safeguarding" and "at risk", without making it entirely clear what the "risk" is, have had the unfortunate effect of confusing child protection with more general child welfare concerns where abuse is not an issue. This confusion has stifled essential debate – after all, who could possibly be against protecting children who are in danger of abuse or serious neglect?'

TERRI DOWTY, Director, ARCH

Contactpoint or 'The Children's Index'

The Contactpoint database, also known as the Children's Index (also known as 'information sharing and assessment' (ISA) or just plain 'IS'; see HMSO (2004)), is being set up under the *Children Act 2004* which gives the Secretary of State for education the power to create a database (or databases) of everyone in England who is aged under 18. It is intended to provide a complete directory of all children from birth, together with a list of the agencies with which they are in contact. It will not hold any case records, but will enable practitioners to contact each other in order to share information: Contactpoint will hold the details of each child's contact with services.

125

The Contactpoint database will cost £224 million to set up and £41 million a year to run. It will be operating in 150 local authorities and be accessible to at least 330,000 users. The database has gone through the pilot phase and will be fully operational by the end of 2008 (Anderson et al. 2006).

There have been significant privacy concerns about the database and much controversy. ARCH said that the proposals invade a child's right to privacy given by the *Convention on the Rights of the Child*, while the Joint Committee on Human Rights said that the 'serious interference' with the rights under Article 8 of the *European Convention on Human Rights*, the right to respect for private life, seems to be 'difficult to justify' (ARCH 2007a).

eCAF

A second database, eCAF, will hold in-depth personal assessment of every child receiving services over and above basic medical care and education, which is an estimated 50% of the child population. The purpose is to allow agencies, including the police, to share data about the child. ARCH (http://www.arch-ed.org/) has voiced concerns on the amount of personal and often sensitive information that will be stored on every child resident in the UK. Further concerns include the practicality of such an initiative. Social services today are stretched for resources on those children that really need help. How these same resources are to engage in creating an in-depth personal assessment on 50% of the child population is yet to be seen.

Online tamper-proof 'online CV' for life

Since February 2008 every 14-year-old child in England has had their exam results and personal details held on a central database. They have each been given a lifelong 'learner number'. The Learning and Skills Council (LSC) insisted it was not a 'tracking system' and would only use existing information that had already been collected 'several times over'. In other words the data exists today in numerous formats located over several digital repositories, hence the move is to consolidate this data into one database. This database will only hold factual information such as first name, surname, age, postcode, qualifications achieved and courses attended according to the LSC, and the system is called Managing Information Across Partners (MIAP).

Did you know that your children's sensitive data will be accessible to 330,000 people? The Contactpoint database, created under the Children Act 2004, will cost £224 million to set up and £41 million a year to run. It will be operating in 150 local authorities and be accessible to at least 330,000 users.

Although pupils in English schools already have a learner number it is currently destroyed when they leave school. The new system will allow students to build up a lifelong record of educational participation. When they leave school it will also allow employers to check their exam results on a tamper-proof 'online CV'.

Did you know that databases and profiling tools have been created to help social services identify those children who show early signs of becoming offenders, and also to share more general concerns about children across a range of agencies: social services, housing services, police, education, health, Connexions (which offers a complete careers, counselling and advice service to 13–19 year olds) and Youth Offending Teams (YOTs). (Each local authority area has its own YOT that is responsible for making provision for youth justice, including preventive work. The YOT is a multi-agency body typically consisting of representatives from police, probation, education and social care. It is answerable to the Youth Justice Board (YJB).)

A significant risk for the future is that the information collected today within controlled usage guidelines will be conveniently enhanced in the future as needs arise, i.e. mission or function creep. There are many examples existing that prove this to be plausible, take the collection of blood samples of all newborn babies in Sweden that is used for research: this was used to identify the assailant in the case of the murder of Anna Lindh the Swedish foreign minister in 2003.

Is your child's DNA among those 100,000 samples from individuals that have never been convicted that GeneWatch estimate are stored in the largest forensic DNA databank in the world? If so, have you tried to get your child's DNA removed?

The Children's Fund

Another initiative called the Children's Fund was launched in November 2000 to tackle disadvantages facing children and young people. The programme aims to identify at an early stage children and young people at risk of social exclusion and make sure that they receive the help and support they need to achieve their potential. However identifying those children that are likely to become offenders when they grow up has its drawbacks. Professor David Farrington FBA (whose work has been used extensively to justify the children's database program) sounds a warning note.

'Caution is, however, required. In particular, any notion that better screening can enable policy makers to identify young children destined to join the 5 per cent of offenders responsible for 50–60 per cent of crime is fanciful. Even if there were no ethical objections to putting "potential delinquent" labels round the necks of young children, there would continue to be statistical barriers. Research into the continuity of anti-social behaviour shows
(Continued)

(Continued)

substantial flows out of – as well as in to – the pool of children who develop chronic conduct problems. This demonstrates the dangers of assuming that anti-social five-year-olds are the criminals or drug abusers of tomorrow, as well as for highlighting the undoubted opportunities that exist for prevention.'

PROFESSOR DAVID FARRINGTON FBA

The tools being developed and used to predict traits of delinquent behaviour in children are the Onset profile (http://www.yjb.gov.uk/en-gb/practitioners/Assessment/Onset.htm) and the RYOGENS (Reducing Youth Offending Generic National Solution) database (Anderson et al. 2006). Onset is used to identify children thought to be 'at risk' of offending. RYOGENS initially focused on the identification of children of any age who were thought to show early signs of becoming offenders, but it is now being developed to share more general concerns about children across a range of agencies: social services, housing services, police, education, health, Connexions and YOTs.

Did you know that the difference between identity theft from a fingerprint and an ID that you may get from your bank is that an ID on a bank card can be changed and the old one deactivated, whereas the same cannot be said about your children's fingerprints?

Tip: Have you checked whether your children's fingerprints (i.e. biometrics) are being stored by their school? If so you may want to consider setting up a parents' lobby group and challenging the schools on the need to use biometrics and how seriously they take the storage of this data, i.e. are the databases secure from unauthorised access?

E-discrimination is a product of 'profiling'. Profiling puts each of our children in groups dependent on characteristics they possess or it can group them by their behaviour. All of this is stored in a database that can be mined. E-discrimination is a system that attempts to predict which children will become delinquent by totting up negative indicators from health, school and other records stored in this database. This information is made available to social workers and any public-sector workers that come into contact with the concerned child. Hence a perfectly law-abiding child coming from a difficult home who has struggled to overcome learning and health difficulties finds active discrimination in that less is expected in the form of achievements and it is almost expected that the child has the odds stacked against them and is likely to offend. In fact one could argue that with e-discrimination you create a self-fulfilling prophecy in that the expectation that the child will offend is more likely to be met.

Loyalty cards and online shopping

Loyalty cards

The subject of the protection of our personal data is not new. A majority of us took out our first loyalty cards (store cards, air-miles etc.) as much as 20 years ago. Loyalty cards give us privileged status with our favourite store, airline etc. Our reward is that we receive special discounts on purchases, express checkout in the supermarket and maybe invitations for special events, free flights, priority upgrading etc. In return the card providers obtain information on us, as consumer demographics: what we buy, how often we buy, where we travel and how often etc. Using this information they may derive statistics regarding the size of household, lifestyle, salary, age, job, number of children and pets etc. We as consumers also receive advertising material that is targeted personally to each of us as an identified consumer group. This can actually feel nice and could give us a feeling of belonging, increased importance and status with the card provider.

Online shopping

The success of the internet has lead to a significant migration of consumer activities from the traditional brick and mortar storefronts to a thriving global ecommerce community. What is different to shopping in a store is that the internet is global and borderless. Hence it is not obvious which country is hosting the server upon which you are shopping. In effect this means that what the other party does with any personal information which you knowingly or unknowingly shared with them is controlled by their business ethics, motivations for collecting information and how they are restricted by the legislation of the hosting country.

1. When you purchase goods online your identity is logged automatically during authentication with what you purchase.
2. If you purchase goods or services everything that is known about you is stored in one of their databases.
3. Whether you identify yourself online or not, how you navigate over the website, i.e. mouse movements, clicks, pages visited etc. maybe logged by using cookies stored on your computer.

Sometimes we will be warned that they are collecting information on us and we may even be given the option to 'opt-out' after reading a long privacy statement. However many of us do not understand or care enough to take assertive action. This means the online store knows who you are, what you purchased and every mouse-click registers you and your household's buying habits. The online store is able to collect even more information on you than is possible with a 'loyalty' card because of this ability to track your online activities. There are no mechanisms available today to enable us, the consumers, to track who is tracking us and to see what, how and where our information is being used. Consequently our private information can become part of the internet, a constituent of a living information pool fuelling those ethical and less-ethical practices found on data collection, sharing and usage. Once our information is out there we have no way of knowing about or controlling its use.

Thus our private information which traditionally only had a value to us has for some time had significant value to others. The privacy implications are as such profound. Information about us, if collected, could end up anywhere in the world and proliferate exponentially during our lifetime.

Data aggregation companies

Companies that specialise in data aggregation include ChoicePoint that won a Big Brother Award in 2006 as the most 'invasive company' (Privacy International 2007). ChoicePoint is a data aggregation company based in the United States that acts as a private intelligence service to government and industry.

ChoicePoint combines personal data sourced from multiple public and private databases for sale to the government and the private sector. The database of personal information contains names, addresses, social security numbers, credit reports and other sensitive data. In 2005 this database contained 250 terabytes of data on 220 million people. In March 2005 it was estimated that the firm maintains more than 17 billion records of individuals and businesses, which it sells to an estimated 100,000 clients, including 7,000 federal, state and local law-enforcement agencies.

Apart from the fact that this data has not been secured sufficiently to prevent theft of data on at least one occasion, the company has also been the subject of lawsuits for maintaining inaccurate data. Choicepoint has in addition been accused of illegally selling the data of overseas citizens to the US government.

Congratulations, you have been profiled

Those that collect personal information on us have the power to profile us. Interested parties that collect our personal information identify which consumer group we belong to with profiling. Profiling is achieved through advanced data-mining techniques, where personal information that is linked directly or indirectly to our identities is collected and mined in a structured way. Profiling by organisations is normally used for retaining customer loyalty, i.e. by customising our buying experience specifically to please us or at least that is how it feels. Amazon.com does this quite effectively by customising our online experience to each of us individually. The online store seems to know what we like by taking our browsing and buying behaviour and using this to work out what we may want to buy next.

Profiling can have an influence on the decisions that we make. In marketing the practices of profiling are normally referred to as behavioural targeting. For example an online company will track a Web visitor's browser clickstreams, typically in the last six or more visits, to predict what the visitor may want in the future and to target ads, content or products based on those personalised past behaviours. In the UK this practice will become even more prevalent once the Phorm systems are operational (see the section later in this chapter on Phorm (UK)).

The Google dance

Google is the world's most popular internet search engine and can legitimately claim to have caused an information and media revolution. The industrious spiderbots that crawl around the web on behalf of Google several times a year in a process referred to as the 'Google dance' sweep through the world's web servers to scrutinise some 8 billion webpages and determine their new rankings in Google's search results. What Google does is use a complex algorithm, but, very simply put, page ranking is determined by the number and importance of pages linking into the page that is being ranked. For example mysecuritybox.blogspot.com (the author's own blog) has two HP websites that link into the blog; this will increase its page ranking. As Google tweaks its ranking algorithms and applies the changes to the pages of the web, different sites shuffle up and down in the search rankings.

Google dances are given names, similarly to hurricanes. The Google dance can often have an impact on the rating of websites in the search results as new algorithms are implemented. There is an ongoing quest to understand how search engines rank websites that has become an obsession for many. There are numerous web forums devoted to the topic that are humming with debate.

Pay-per-click advertising

Internet advertising is booming and is expected to continue growing significantly. The biggest category is 'pay-per-click' advertising. How it works is that advertisers bid on keywords that they believe potential customers will be interested in. This enables search engines such as Google and Yahoo! to display advertisements alongside the results of search queries. So if you were to search for a particular wine it is likely that you will be presented with adverts from wine merchants.

Google and Yahoo! also place adverts on affiliated websites, for our wine example this could be a wine appreciation society. The advertiser only pays when a user clicks on an ad. It is also becoming increasingly common for bloggers to place ads on their pages. MySpace is an advertising playground. All blogs have the potential to be 'monitised' with the addition of banner ads, the result being that bloggers earn a small commission each time somebody visits their page and clicks on the ad. Heather Armstrong did this (see the section 'Your blog as your personal diary or money-making machine') and over time the advertising revenue from her blog has become the main source of her family's income. Hence now there is starting to be real money in the business of blogging as every major consumer advertiser realises that if you can engage effectively with these newly networked hordes, then they become agents of your brand.

The benefit of pay-per-click ads over traditional advertising is that advertisers reach a better quality of leads. On the downside click-fraud within pay-per-click advertising is a growing nuisance. Click-fraud is bogus clicks that do not come from genuinely interested customers. There are two main forms of click-fraud.

1. If you click repeatedly on the ads on your website or get other people or machines to do so on your behalf, then you can generate a stream of bogus commissions.
2. Click-fraud can also be used by one company against another and repeatedly clicking on a rival firm's ads can create a huge bill.

A successor to the pay-per-click advertising is the newly pioneered pay-per-action: a new model whereby advertisers only pay if a click on an ad is followed by an action such as a purchase or a download.

Advertising goes mobile

It seems that advertisers are getting pretty excited about the potential of the mobile phone. This is no surprise when you consider that cellular carriers possess terabytes of demographic data on their users and they even know where the caller is. Your mobile phone gives all of this away. Advertisers today have the potential to mould campaigns that can be aimed at specific age, gender, income and lifestyle segments and locations. This is bringing advertisers around the world close to their long dreamed of vision: the mobile phone as an ultimate, targeted, personal marketing machine.

Advertisers today are working out how best to leverage this to its fullest potential. With consumers still not enthusiastic at purchasing entertainment on their phones, advertisers are running banner ads and giving away videos and games that display their products. BMW, Adidas and Gillette all make short, branded films that South Korea's largest telecom operator SK Telecom distributes for free.

Social networking

Another part of information privacy that is not covered by any legal framework is the information that we are sharing when we go online. This raises a whole new connotation to the definition of 'information exposure' in the domain of information security when applied within the context of social networking. 'Information exposure' is normally the consequence of malicious or accidental activity when information that should be kept private, i.e. secure from unauthorised access, becomes exposed. However online in the social networking spaces individuals are publishing private information on themselves, their families, their friends on the web knowingly and willingly, although they are perhaps naive to the potential risks. This information is unstructured in how it is organised and may or may not be linked to their identity. 'Digital information residue' is our personal information that has been collected or shared and digitally stored somewhere by someone or something in cyberspace and over which we have no control. See Chapter 2 for some insight into what is really going on out there.

BODILY PRIVACY

The collection of DNA is in the area of 'bodily privacy' as defined by Privacy International (2006b), along with body and cavity searches. This section takes a dive into the recent growing practice of the collection of DNA that is happening in almost every country in the world.

The UK has the largest forensic DNA databank in the world. In this databank there are approximately 100,000 children that are 'innocent' in that they have not even received a caution after being arrested.

Can you imagine a world whereby the DNA of every person alive (and many that are dead) is stored in a databank somewhere? The implications are profound and irreversible, as it links every one of us to our unique identifier that is an intrinsic part of our makeup. Do you believe in the argument of 'nothing to hide, hence nothing to fear'? Do you see this as a good justification for why we should share our DNA? Ask this question to yourself now and then again when you have finished reading this section.

What is DNA?

'Each person's DNA, with the exception of identical twins, is different from that of every other human being. Genetic data poses unique privacy issues because it can serve as an identifier and can also convey sensitive personal information. Not only does genetic information provide something like a fingerprint through variations in genetic sequences; it also provides a growing amount of information about genetic diseases and predispositions. Errors in the genetic code are responsible for an estimated 3,000 to 4,000 hereditary diseases. Genetic alterations increase a person's risk of developing that disorder. The disease itself results from the interaction of such genetic predispositions and environmental factors, including diet and lifestyle. In addition to indicating predisposition to disease, studies conducted do infer that genes do play a role to influence behaviour. Although the findings are inconclusive, genes have been found to influence homosexuality, depressive tendencies, thrill-seeking and tendencies towards violent criminal behaviour in genetics research studies.'

US HUMAN GENOME PROJECT

Begun formally in 1990 the US Human Genome Project was a 13-year effort coordinated by the US Department of Energy and the National Institutes of Health. The project originally was planned to last 15 years, but rapid technological advances accelerated the completion date to 2003. Project goals were to (ORNL 2008):

- identify all of the approximately 20,000–25,000 genes in human DNA;
- determine the sequences of the 3 billion chemical base pairs that make up human DNA;

- store this information in databases;
- improve tools for data analysis;
- transfer related technologies to the private sector; and
- address the ethical, legal and social issues (ELSI) that may arise from the project.

The growth of DNA databanks

The popular US television series CSI gives to us a very clear picture on the importance of DNA in law enforcement. Although the stories are fabricated they are based on real types of cases. CSI gives us an insight into how DNA is used in criminology. In the real world law-enforcement agencies worldwide are becoming increasingly reliant on DNA evidence. Offenders today can be convicted purely on evidence provided by DNA. One famous example in Sweden is the conviction of the murderer of Anna Lindh. Although the analysis of DNA is traditionally used to prove guilt there is nonetheless a growing trend for the use of DNA to prove innocence in the elimination of suspects. The consequences are that the growth of DNA databanks is not only due to those people convicted of some crime but also those who are innocent.

'The United Kingdom has the largest forensic DNA databank in the world. Since April 4, 2004, those who have been arrested but not charged are also included in the databank, as are those arrested for drunk driving, even if not convicted. The UK Police National DNA Database was set up in 1995, initially to store the profiles of those convicted of crimes. Acts of Parliament in 2001 and 2004 gradually extended police powers to take and keep DNA samples from anyone arrested on suspicion of committing a "recordable" offence (which means most offences) – even if they were released without charge or acquitted by a court. Since this legislation, there has been a rapid expansion of the databank to its current

(Continued)

(Continued)
**level of more than 4.2 [million] profiles, and of these
700,000 belong to children and 30 of them are under
10 years old.'**

PRIVACY INTERNATIONAL, 2006b

Until 1998 a child aged 10–14 was presumed '*doli incapax*',
i.e. not to have sufficient maturity to be guilty of a crime.
The *Crime and Disorder Act 1998* removed that presumption.
Now, any child in England and Wales aged 10 or over can be
arrested on suspicion of a criminal offence. In Scotland, the
age is 8 (although in practice young children will be dealt
with through the Scottish panel system rather than the judicial
system).

Did you know that in Sweden almost every citizen born
in 1975 or later has provided a blood sample at birth for
the purpose of research? Function or mission creep has
recently resulted in these blood samples being used
for the conviction of a murderer in 2003 and for identification of victims from the Tsunami disaster in Thailand
in 2004.

The policy of retaining the DNA profiles of people who have
not been convicted or cautioned for any offence has caused
huge controversy, particularly where children and young
teenagers are concerned. No other country in Europe crimi-
nalises children at such a young age; no other country in the
world has such an extensive DNA database.

It is expected that nearly 1.5 million 10–18 year olds will
have been entered on the national DNA database by Spring
2009. GeneWatch (http://www.genewatch.co.uk) calculates
that some 100,000 children on the database are 'innocent' in
that they have not even received a caution after being arrested.
It also claims that between 1995 and 2007 only 189 minors

have successfully applied to have their details taken off the register.

In the US trends are also towards the expansion of DNA databanks. The DNA of more than 80,000 people is added every month. Each of the 50 states has a DNA databank of some kind and each collects and enters information regarding all persons convicted of sex crimes and most felonies. The state and federal laws for collection of DNA have broadened considerably in recent years. In addition to collecting information on violent felons, DNA of those committing misdemeanours and juvenile offenders is now being collected in more than half of the states.

Did you know that all 27 EU countries agreed to unrestricted access to genetic information, fingerprints and car registration information in all EU police databases?

In New Zealand newborn blood spot samples and related information is collected and this data may be used by the police, but only as a last resort or with parental consent. In the city of Bristol, UK, a pilot project is underway to collect DNA samples from 25,000 babies and their parents as part of a national DNA database that could be used for law enforcement. Furthermore a proposal is being considered on whether to expand the collection of DNA without consent for purposes of identification.

Several countries are building nationwide DNA databases for medical research driven principally by pharmaceutical companies and other business enterprises hoping to profit from new medical procedures and services. Medical research is the driver in Sweden whereby almost every citizen born in 1975 or later has provided a blood sample at birth (PKU-laboratoriet 2008). The sample is used to test for a genetic disease Phenyle–Ketone–Uria (PKU). It is also saved for future medical research in a database. The database does not contain any DNA profiles, but the blood samples can easily be analysed. There is also identity data provided with each sample. The database is not intended for use in criminal investigation. However in the high-profile case of the murder of Anna Lindh (the Swedish secretary of foreign affairs) the police obtained temporary access to the database which was used to identify the murderer. A short time later there was a slight modification to the Swedish law to enable the data-bank to be used to identify the 543 victims (The Local 2005) of the Asian Tsunami disaster in Thailand on 26 December 2004.

The Prüm Treaty

'The aim of the Treaty is to help the signatories improve information-sharing for the purpose of preventing and combating crime in three fields, all of which are covered by provisions of EU Treaty: terrorism, cross-border crime and illegal migration.'

The Treaty of Prüm and the Principle of Loyalty

In December 2006 Germany and Austria became the first countries in the world to match their DNA databases. Using a hit/no-hit procedure police officers retrieving the data are informed whether or not data on the profile in question is also contained in the database of the other participating state. Following a successful hit the police officers then get in touch with the other force to request mutual legal assistance in order to obtain more detailed information on the identity of the person concerned.

The Prüm Treaty (CHALLENGE 2006) signed between Germany and Austria is the core of a system that today also includes Belgium, Spain, France, Luxembourg and the Netherlands. In addition Italy, Sweden, Greece, Slovenia, Finland, Bulgaria and Romania have all said that they will join the scheme and the Germany–Austria data-sharing model will be expanded in the coming year to some of these countries. The Treaty makes automatic the sharing of certain kinds of information. Vehicle registration, DNA analysis and fingerprint records are all automatically searchable as are entire profiles of people.

On 13 June 2007 all 27 EU countries agreed to unrestricted access to genetic information, fingerprints and car registration information in all EU police databases. Thus police in one EU country will be able to enter a suspect's genetic data into a database and obtain matches for any other EU country as well. The new system will also feature the sharing of fingerprints and pictures for non-EU citizens seeking visas to enter Europe. The system can store the data for up to 70 million people (Privacy International 2008d). It has been hailed as a way to tackle immigration issues and transnational crime.

Using DNA testing to discriminate

The two most controversial areas of genetic testing are in the workplace and in the provision of medical and life insurance. Psychological tests, general intelligence tests, performance tests, personality tests, honesty and background checks, drug tests and medical tests are routinely used in workplace recruitment and evaluation methods. Since the discovery of DNA and especially since completion of the Human Genome Project (ORNL 2008) there has been an increased use of genetic testing, allowing employers to access the most intimate details of a person's makeup in order to predict susceptibility to diseases as well as medical or even behavioural conditions.

As genetic databases become more common worldwide there has been a concurrent rise in the use of testing by employers. Although there are legitimate uses of genetic testing, such as the prevention of occupational diseases, there is also concern that employers will use these tests to discriminate against current or potential employees, for example whether someone is prone to mental or physical disorders (e.g. depression). Currently genetic testing is prohibitively expensive for many employers and not used as frequently as other forms of medical or drug testing.

> Article 21 of the *European Union Charter of Fundamental Rights* provides explicitly that 'any discrimination based on . . . genetic features . . . shall be prohibited.'

While often tied to the workplace in the United States, where employers often provide and pay for health insurance, genetic testing has also been directly used in the underwriting of life and medical insurance. In February 2001 Norwich Union Life, one of Britain's largest insurers, admitted using genetic tests for breast and ovarian cancer and Alzheimer's disease to evaluate applicants (Privacy International 2008e). They were in fact violating the industry's code of conduct since the genetic tests have not been approved by the government's Human Genetics Commission. The consequences of the test results were that some individuals paid higher insurance premiums. This created political pressure in the UK to outlaw the use of genetic data by insurers.

There are many examples provided in this section that illustrate the potential risks associated with the collection and storage of DNA. Apart from the pure security aspect, there is the risk of mission or function creep, making any DNA collected the source of advanced data-mining techniques. We can speculate on what happens if collected DNA is used to profile us in the future. Will the use of DNA overstep the boundaries of what is considered acceptable use of DNA? What is the next step? Give our DNA to insurance companies or to our employers? Could it be that the erosion will happen so transparently that we will not even notice it happening?

PRIVACY OF COMMUNICATIONS

The practice of wiretapping is prevalent in the United States and some other countries such as China and Saudi Arabia. Most countries around the world however do regulate the interception of communications that take the form of constitutional provisions. In contrast these laws are also in response to law-enforcement and intelligence agency pressure to increase surveillance capabilities. Countries such as Australia, Belgium, Germany, New Zealand, South Africa and the UK have all updated their laws to facilitate surveillance of new technologies.

US wiretapping practices

The US government has led a worldwide effort to limit individual privacy and enhance the capability of its police and intelligence services to eavesdrop on personal conversations. The *Communications Assistance for Law Enforcement Act* (CALEA) sets out legal requirements for telecommunications providers and equipment manufacturers on the surveillance capabilities that must be built into all telephone systems used in the United States. At the time of writing ISPs in the United States are exempted, but change is on the way. The FBI is calling for the Federal Communications Commission to expand the law to reconsider Voice over IP (VoIP) and classify ISPs as telecommunications carriers under CALEA. If these providers are reclassified as carriers, then the requirements for intercept capability under CALEA will also apply to them.

Wiretapping practices worldwide

Many of the international laws on wiretapping date back to a series of seminars hosted by the FBI in the United States in 1993 at its research facility in Quantico, Virginia, called the *International Law Enforcement Telecommunications Seminar* (ILETS) together with representatives from Canada, Hong Kong, Australia and the EU. The product of these meetings was the adoption of an international standard called the *International Requirements for Interception* that possessed similar characteristics to CALEA from the United States. In 1995 the Council of the European Union approved a secret resolution adopting the ILETS. Following its adoption and without revealing the role of the FBI in developing the standard, many countries have adopted laws to this effect. Following adoption of the standard the European Union and the United States offered a Memorandum of Understanding (MoU) for other countries to sign to commit to the standards. All participating countries were encouraged to adopt the standards so it was natural that international standards organisations, such as the International Telecommunications Union (ITU) and the European Telecommunication Standardization Institute (ETSI), would adopt the standards.

International wiretapping laws

Australia was one of the first countries to sign the MoU along with Canada. In Australia the *Telecommunications Act* expects the telecommunications operators to proactively assist law enforcement by providing an interception capability.

In the UK RIPA requires that telecommunications operators maintain a 'reasonable interception capability' in their systems and be able to provide on notice certain 'traffic data'.

In the Netherlands all ISPs have to have the capability to intercept all traffic with a court order and maintain users' logs for three months.

In New Zealand the *Telecommunications (Interception Capabilities) Act 2004* obliges telecommunications companies and ISPs to intercept phone calls and emails on the request of the police and security services.

In Switzerland ISPs are required to take all necessary measures to allow for the interception of mail and telecommunications.

The wiretapping law (FRA-lagen) in Sweden

In June 2008 Sweden's parliament approved controversial new laws allowing authorities to spy on cross-border email and telephone traffic. The Swedish press claim that this will make Sweden the most surveyed country in Europe.

This wiretapping law enables the intelligence authorities to 'listen' to all traffic, Hotmail, MSN, SMS etc., across Sweden's borders. The law becomes effective at the end of 2009. Given Sweden's stance on human rights the passing of this law is quite remarkable. It was following some pretty heated discussions in parliament that the law was passed on a very fine majority (47 against and 52 for). The argument for tapping of international lines is 'terrorism'. Of course any 'terrorists' will encrypt their communications and there is nothing that the Swedish authorities can do about this. Of course one can always monitor 'traffic patterns' on identified suspect communication which can be as revealing as the communications' contents themselves in certain situations. However the use of the contents of such communications in a court of law will be impossible without the decryption key and they cannot obtain this unless there is a law enacted similar to the RIPA in the UK, which forces the key-holder to give the encryption or decryption key to the authorities on request and if they refuse they can be convicted for concealing evidence.

Phorm (UK)

During 2008 there has been a growing controversy about interception of people's web traffic in the UK. At the centre of the storm is the 'patent-pending' technology of a new company called Phorm. The drivers behind this are not government authorities but three of the main players in the telecommunications space.

BT, TalkTalk and Virgin have all signed up to use Phorm, which targets adverts to users based on users' web browsing habits. Phorm's proprietary ad serving technology claims to use anonymised ISP data to deliver the right ad to the right person at the right time, the right number of times. This means that end-users will receive advertising that is tailored to their interests in real time. Keywords in websites visited by a user are scanned and connected to advertising categories and then matched to particular adverts. That data may include sensitive personal data, because it will include the search terms entered by users into search engines and these can easily reveal information about such matters as political opinions, sexual proclivities, religious views and health.

> If a user is given a random persistent ID by the Phorm product, this means that whenever the user accesses the ISP, the ISP can see the link between the assigned ID and the user's natural identity.

Phorm anonymises identities: each user is given a persistent random ID, so that each time they browse, the same ID is used to collect information on their habits over a period of time, but Phorm cannot see the link between this ID and the natural identity. Phorm uses the ID to deliver tailored advertisements in their browser. This ID is used to distinguish the user from the millions of others on the internet and it does not contain any information about the user themselves or their computer. Users will have the choice to opt-in or opt-out of this service. TalkTalk has said it intends to make Phorm an opt-in system, whilst as of Spring 2008 the two other ISPs had not yet decided.

If a user is given a persistent ID, this means that whenever the user accesses the ISP, the ISP can see the link between the assigned ID and the user's natural identity. The persistent ID is not encrypted as it is in the form of a cookie. To ensure 'separation of duty' the system will enable the ISPs to prevent Phorm from knowing the user's natural identity. This means that the ISPs will hold the persistent ID assigned to natural users and Phorm will receive the browsing habits attached to the persistent ID. If this is the case one could argue that the Phorm system is not based on anonymity, but it is in reality based on controlling the release of information.

Let us pretend that this is no problem and that there also exists legislation to ensure that the ISP and Phorm can never have the chance to match the users browsing habits to a natural identity. Many users will in any case be identifiable from the content of the data scanned, since it will include email sent or retrieved by users of web-based email and messages viewable by those authorised to gain access to individual pages of social networking sites.

According to an open letter sent to the UK Information Commissioner on 17 March 2008 (Fipr 2008), the Foundation for Information Policy Research[4] have claimed that the online advert system Phorm is illegal and contravenes RIPA.

> 'The need for both parties to consent to interception in order for it to be lawful is an extremely basic principle within the legislation, and it cannot be lightly ignored or treated as a technicality.'
>
> NICHOLAS BOHM, general counsel at Fipr

Fipr believes Phorm contravenes the *Data Protection Act*, in that users have to opt-out rather than opt-in, and RIPA, which makes the interception of any transmission across a public telecommunication system illegal without the explicit consent of users. (Exceptions are when police are investigating a serious crime such as kidnapping and need to listen in to conversations between a family and the criminals, although even they must first obtain an authorisation under RIPA.)

If you want to avoid having your online habits tracked you need to find out first if your provider is using the Phorm system as opt-in or opt-out. If you need to opt-out be aware that when you clear the cookies in your browser, you will need to go through the process of opting-out again.

Although from a privacy standpoint Phorm's technology is very bad, from other perspectives what they are offering is quite nice. It will mean that you should not receive adverts on products and services that you are just not interested in and it could make your online experiences more pleasant. The end-user experience will be similar to that at amazon.com and other popular online stores which as a matter of course drop cookies onto your PC for the purpose of tracking your shopping experience.

Privacy in the workplace

Traditionally monitoring and information gathering in the workplace involved some form of human intervention and either the consent or at least the knowledge of employees. The changing structure and nature of the workplace however has led to more invasive and often covert monitoring practices which call into question employees' most basic rights to privacy and dignity within the workplace. Progress in technology has facilitated an increasing level of automated surveillance. Now the supervision of employee performance, behaviour and communications can be carried out by technological means, with increased ease and efficiency. The technology currently being developed is extremely powerful and can extend to every aspect of a worker's life. Software programs can record key-strokes on computers and capture screen images, telephone management systems can analyse the pattern of telephone use and the destination of calls, and miniature cameras and 'Smart' ID badges can monitor an employee's behaviour, movements and even physical orientation. Unfortunately privacy laws in relation to workplace privacy vary quite significantly between countries and in a few countries there are minimal legal constraints when it comes to workplace surveillance. For example in the United States they do not seem to understand what it means to have the right for privacy in the workplace: it is assumed that as employers have ownership or 'control' over the working premises and its contents and facilities, that employees give up all rights and expectations to privacy and freedom from invasion. Other employers ensure that the employees consent to surveillance, monitoring and testing as a condition of employment.

In European countries the *EU Data Protection Directive* and the *Telecommunication Privacy Directive* control the collection and processing of personal information. The problem is that they only cover the confidentiality of public systems, not the private systems owned by our employers. This means that their application to workplace privacy issues is not always clear. In May 2002 the European Union Article 29 Data Protection Working Party issued a working paper on monitoring and surveillance of electronic communications in the workplace. The document set out principles employers should bear in mind when processing workers' personal data. For example any data collected must be collected for a specific and legitimate purpose, there should be some transparency in that workers should know which data the employer is collecting about them and the employer must implement security measures at the workplace to ensure the safety of the personal data of workers that has been collected and is stored somewhere.

Good examples of how legislation has been rolled out to protect workplace privacy can be found in Finland and Belgium. Finland has a new law on *Data Protection in Working Life* that entered into force in October 2004. The law includes: the prohibition of routine drug tests, restrictions on the right to video surveillance and the guarantee of limited email privacy for workers. In Belgium there is a national collective agreement that protects employee online privacy.

TERRITORIAL PRIVACY

Big brother or a little brother/sister state?

However quickly privacy regulations are agreed between participating countries and codified as law, surveillance seems to be growing on an endemic scale. The race is on and the slow grinding wheels of bureaucracy are losing. It is easy to speculate with some accuracy whether we really are 'sleepwalking into a surveillance society' as predicted by the UK Information Commissioner, Richard Thomas in 2004 (Surveillance Studies Network 2006).

We can take this a step further and question whether we will wake up tomorrow in an Orwellian society (Orwell 1949). The Royal Academy of Engineering (2007) published a report whereby they likened this development to a 'little brother society'. In effect they state that what we are seeing is not really a big brother society (i.e. Orwellian) but something that possesses the characteristics of a 'little brother/sister' society notable by the fact that the surveillance is disparate and disconnected. There is no central governing body that has ultimate authority to see and control everything that is tracked.

In addition to surveillance performed by government authorities, it is other interested parties that have their own motivations for wanting to know us better. Then of course you have surveillance cameras that are installed just to demonstrate due diligence[5] to insurance brokers etc. These cameras are not normally high-tech, producing images that are of negligible quality that rarely could be used as evidence in a court of law.

According to Privacy International (2006b) tracking and surveillance technologies can be subdivided into three categories. First are the active location-tracking technologies which include mobile phones, wireless internet devices and automobile location technologies. Second are passive technologies that include biometric sensors, surveillance cameras with recognition software and RFID technology. Third are those technologies that have the unintended consequence of tracking location information, such as the recording of a point-of-sale transaction. Location information may be collected in the provision of location-based services (LBS) or as a necessary part of some other service as shown by the third category, point-of-sale transactions. For example if you pay for some goods at the supermarket using your credit card, you are recorded by default at being at that location at that point in time by the time-stamp on the credit card transaction.

Surveillance

Surveillance cameras or CCTV (Figure 5.2) are increasingly being used to monitor public and private spaces throughout the world. Governments and law-enforcement authorities, companies and private individuals use video surveillance for the prevention of crimes, the safety of urban environments

FIGURE 5.2   *CCTV*

and government buildings, traffic control, the monitoring of demonstrators and in the context of criminal investigations. Surveillance technologies have even been described as the 'fifth utility' (Graham 2002) where CCTV is being integrated into the urban environment in much the same way as the electricity supply and the telephone network in the first half of the century.

Surveillance cameras can comprise linked systems with diverse functions such as full pan (a 'full panoramic' view can be achieved by rotating the lens or stitching images together), tilt, zoom and night vision or infrared capability. Cameras with audio capability also exist, so for example if a drunk in a public space knocks over a dustbin, the camera operator has the capability to request that the drunk places it back: almost Orwellian.

There is a growing trend in the creation of rings of steel around key cities or parts of cities whereby all entrances to the city are monitored, e.g. vehicles with their number plates and drivers are photographed. The most publicised is around central London and in New York where they are planning the 'Lower Manhattan Security Initiative'. You may have also noticed a growing momentum for the use of CCTV in schools and nurseries.

Many countries have their own laws concerning the use of video cameras, for example Privacy International (2006b) reported that the Greek Data Protection Commissioner issued a directive prohibiting the use of CCTV, except in certain circumstances. In Sweden the 1998 *Law on Secret Camera Surveillance* restricts the use of video surveillance: despite this the proliferation of CCTV in public places, schools and even in taxis has become commonplace. Government authorities justify the use of cameras in the fight against terrorism and crime, so we are being propelled into a future surveillance society, driven by influential countries such as Britain and the United States.

> 'Surveillance in Britain has now reached a level equivalent to Russia and Malaysia. If something is not done soon to reverse this trend, privacy will be extinct within a decade.'
>
> SIMON DAVIES, director of Privacy International, 2007

Britain has by far the most surveillance cameras in the world: about 1 for every 12 people or approximately 5 million in public and private hands. In addition a 2006 ranking of 37 countries by Privacy International found that the UK level of surveillance was endemic, being higher than any other EU country and at the same level as Russia, China and Singapore. We can anticipate that in 10 years time surveillance will be all-pervasive in the UK and many other key countries around the world. New surveillance technologies with improved intelligence are rapidly being developed.

What about a transparent society?

Let us take a look at surveillance from another viewpoint. What happens if we live in a society whereby we are all tracking each other? Could this bring some benefits, e.g. force accountability in everything we and those in positions of power do? Brin (1998) takes the analogy of a 'tale of two cities' supposedly of the future. In this analogy he gives you a choice to live in one of the cities and to help you make the choice he describes them as follows.

'At first sight these two municipalities look pretty much alike. Both contain dazzling technological marvels, especially in the realm of electronic media. Both suffer from familiar urban quandaries of frustration and decay. If some progress is being made in solving human problems, it is happening gradually. Perhaps some kids seem better educated. The air may be marginally cleaner. People still worry about overpopulation, the environment and the next international crisis.

None of these features is of interest to us right now, for we have noticed something about both of these twenty-first-century cities that is radically different. A trait that marks them as distinct from any metropolis of the late 1990s. Street crime has nearly vanished from both towns. But that is only a symptom, a result.

The real change peers down from every lamppost, every rooftop and street sign. Tiny cameras, panning left and right, survey traffic and pedestrians, observing everything in open view. Have we entered an Orwellian nightmare? Have the burghers of both towns banished muggings at the cost of creating a Stalinist dystropia?

Consider city number one. In this place, all the myriad cameras report their urban scenes straight to the Police Centre, where security officers use sophisticated image processors to scan for infractions against public order – or perhaps against an established way of thought. Citizens walk the streets aware that any word or deed may be noted by agents of some mysterious bureau.

At first sight, things seem quite similar in city number two. Again, ubiquitous cameras perch on every vantage point.

(Continued)

(Continued)

Only here we soon find a crucial difference. These devices do not report to the secret police. Rather, each and every citizen of this metropolis can use his or her wristwatch television to call up images from any camera in town. Here a late-evening stroller checks to make sure no one lurks beyond the corner she is about to turn. Over there a tardy young man dials to see if his dinner date still waits for him by a city fountain. A block away, an anxious parent scans the area to find which way her child wandered off. Over by the mall, a teenage shoplifter is taken into custody gingerly with minute attention to ritual and rights, because the arresting officer knows that the entire process is being scrutinized by untold numbers who watch intently, lest her neutral professionalism lapse. In city number two, such microcameras are banned from some indoor places . . . but not from police headquarters! There any citizen may tune in on bookings, arrangements, and especially the camera control room itself, making sure that the agents on duty look out for violent crime and only crime.'

DAVID BRIN, 1998

So Brin gives us a choice of two cities within which we can chose to live: they are similar in that they have similar levels of crime and lifestyle; however the differences lie in that the first is almost Orwellien with government authorities controlling city-wide surveillance whereas the other has everyone tracking everyone else, i.e. sousveillance.

So if we take the little brother society and add to this the growing practice of 'sousveillence', i.e. we are tracking each other, nobody has any secrets, 'if you want to know anything about me then tell me what I want to know about you', then this takes us into what David Brin refers to as a 'transparent society'.

Sousveillence

The practice of 'sousveillence' has been enacted in real life for some years now by Steve Mann, who claims to be the world's first cyborg. Apparently he walks around every day of his life with a camera and recording devices strapped to his head as could be the case if we evolve into an evidencary-based society in the future. His devices called 'life recorders' (also called a 'glogger') were originally large and imposing, however they have over the years become more sophisticated and smaller.

An evidencary-based society would make us feel obliged to keep a life recorder on our person 24/7 days a week. The life recorder could comprise CCTV and a recording device or maybe just a recording device alone. It would be used in cases where 'we need to prove our innocence'. This is not so far-fetched; it is just a matter of time before police officers are using these as a standard tool in their work. Just as it has become the norm today to provide DNA evidence to prove our innocence, so will it be the case with the 'life recorder'.

Surveillance and sousveillance clearly have some benefits as well as those less desirable effects highlighted in this book. If we have no choice for the future, then we can speculate on how best to optimise this growing trend for the benefit of the people, i.e. if the government or organisations collect information on us, wherever we may live in the world, we should have the right to know what has been collected and how it is being used. We should have the right to demand 'transparency' from the government, i.e. they must also have no secrets from their citizens.

ID cards

ID cards are in use in one form or another in virtually all countries of the world. The type of card, its functions and integrity vary enormously. While several countries have official, compulsory, national ID cards that are used for a variety of purposes, many countries do not. Having said that, just because the ID card is non-compulsory does not necessarily mean that you can function effectively in the country without one. An example is Sweden where the ID card is not compulsory but to live and work in the country without one is almost impossible, as it is the official means with which to present your personal

ID number[6] that is requested in many everyday transactions. However it is successful and Swedish residents today could not imagine living in a society without it. An ID card with a unique identifier has proved to be very convenient.

Nevertheless not many countries are like Sweden and proposals to establish national ID cards have invariably sparked protests in many countries including the UK. Groups such as the No2ID campaign (http://www.no2id.net/IDSchemes/) and Privacy International have been fighting against the National Identity Management System proposed by the UK government. If implemented the architecture will include a national identity register (NIR) holding personal information and biometric data of all British citizens. This is effectively an identity management system (see Figure 5.3) that will function as a hub to

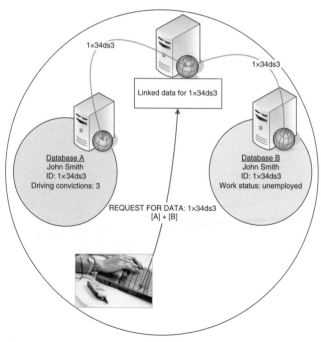

FIGURE 5.3   *An example of an identity management system*

other connected government databases. This means that any authenticated government official will potentially have the capability to access all information contained within the database if they are authorised. Whether they are authorised is important because this is very much dependent on how effective the business processes implemented today and planned for the future are in determining who should have access to what. What are the rules? What are the exceptions? This is like placing all your eggs in one basket with only one lock and key and then having one guardian that decides who should have access to which eggs based upon pre-agreed business rules, as opposed to having many baskets of eggs each with their own lock and key and each having their own guardian.

The problem is not just the linking of the databases, it is also that if existing business processes are flawed, so too will the implementation of any technology such as identity management. In fact flawed business processes normally succeed in bringing these flaws to the surface in ways that could cause the government embarrassment and further loss of trust from UK citizens.

An example of how an identity management architecture could look is shown in Figure 5.3. The linking of databases makes sensitive information that is today distributed over several locations more readily available. The consequences are that it will be possible for our personal data to be mined (data-mining is used to find patterns in data held in databases, normally referred as data-warehousing; examples of the results of data-mining include identifying which proportion of customers are pet owners, are vegetarian, are over 50 years old, are pensioners etc.) at the click of a key through one access point. The risk lies in the fact that it will take only one person with the right access to any of the planned databases (that are linked) to be careless or corrupt and then the whole country's records become vulnerable.

Although several expert reports have been released explaining the perils of such a national identity system, including some from the London School of Economics, the UK government is determined to find a creative method by which to implement the NIR. One approach that has been suggested is the creation of biometric visas and ID cards for non-citizens, and this has been initiated with the news in the beginning of 2008 of the compulsory issue of biometric ID cards for all immigrants by the end of 2008. The government do not foresee any significant protests against this as most British are in favour of improved clampdowns on immigrants. There is also a drive to ensure that all students are issued with an ID card. As these cards provide evidence that the person is over 18 years of age there will be minimal resistance (18 years is the legal age when young people can drink alcohol in the UK).

There are several countries that have tried and failed to implement ID card systems. For example the Philippine Supreme Court ruled that a national ID system violated the constitutional right to privacy in 1998, a year earlier the Portuguese Constitution stated that 'Citizens shall not be given an all-purpose national identity number' and back in 1991 the Hungarian Constitutional Court ruled that a law creating a multi-use personal identification number violated the constitutional right of privacy.

Severe lobbying and massive protests against uniform ID card initiatives have lead to the near collapse of some governments. The Australia Card in 1987 is one example. Now Australia is debating legislation to implement an Access Card that is supposedly meant to replace 17 different identity cards used for a variety of government applications, including disability, unemployment and healthcare, in effect a repackaged ID card. Critics such as the Australian Privacy Foundation and Electronic Frontiers Australia are fighting the implementation of the Access Card. Another project in progress in Australia is that they have been busy compiling a massive database, including biometric data, linked to identity documents for non-citizens, the same as in the UK. In other countries opposition to the cards combined with the high economic cost and other logistical difficulties of implementing the systems has led to their withdrawal. Card projects in South Korea and Taiwan were stopped after widespread protests. In the United States plans to convert the state driver's license into a nationwide system of identification have stalled because of the stiff resistance from a broad coalition of civil society groups. Although the *REAL ID Act* (Privacy International 2008d) was passed in the United States in May 2005, states and public organisations have rebelled against the scheme. Sixteen states have passed legislation rejecting the *REAL ID Act* and there are also bills in both US legislative houses that would repeal the Act creating the national identification system. Hundreds of organisations have expressed concerned with the bill and it still seems unlikely that the *Real ID Act* will be implemented in the United States.

Perhaps if these governments were to take some of the rules concerning the management of their citizens personal data from Kim Cameron's (Kim Cameron works for Microsoft and is a respected guru in the identity space; his blog can be found at http://www.identityblog.com/) 'Principles on Identity' (*The Economist*, 16 February 2008) they could at least start to earn some respect from their constituents.

1. Start from the principle that users may be identified only with their (or their parents') explicit consent.
2. Information minimisation is that only that information that is needed is kept, information should not be kept 'just in case'.
3. Identity systems must be able to check who is asking for the information and not just hand it over.

In fact from a practical perspective a national ID scheme and linking of databases has many advantages for the citizen if implemented correctly, i.e. security mechanisms implemented that ensure that personal data is protected from unauthorised access and modification. It is not just the government that benefits.

Such an example can be provided by Sweden whereby every newborn is provided with a personal ID. This is used throughout their lives. This unique identifier has in recent years facilitated the linking of health records, which means that if you end up in accident and emergency one day, by checking your personal ID the staff treating you are able pull up your health records and make better informed decisions, so as to have a better chance of saving your life in extreme situations.

In general the Swedish people trust their government. The national identifier in Sweden is a 'no brainer'. It is practical and makes life easier for everyone concerned. The trust for the government has been earned by years of a socialistic regime that has demonstrated a serious approach when it comes to taking care of its people. However one should bear in mind that Sweden has a population of only 9 million, so the system seems to work although it is not perfect. To get the same principle working in the UK with a population of 64 million is moving to another level: it is the difference between preparing to run a 10 km race and a marathon.

Border controls

The USA Patriot Act

The use of RFID and biometrics in passports is growing despite impassioned public resistance, a trend triggered primarily by the United States after 9/11 and the passing of a couple of Acts that have changed the make-up of the passport as was then used. The most well-known act was the *USA Patriot Act* and another less known act the *Enhanced Border Security and Visa Entry Reform Act 2002*. The second law necessitated international cooperation. The incentive was made clear as follows.

'By October 26, 2004, in order for a country to remain eligible for participation in the visa waiver program its government must certify that it has a program to issue to its nationals machine-readable passports that are tamper-resistant and which incorporate biometric and authentication identifiers that satisfy the standards of the International Civil Aviation Organization (ICAO).'

Enhanced Border Security and
Visa Entry Reform Act 2002

These laws gave momentum to the standards that were being considered at the International Civil Aviation Organization

(ICAO) by requiring visa waiver countries (which include many EU countries, Australia, Brunei, Iceland, Japan, Monaco, New Zealand, Norway, Singapore and Slovenia) to implement biometrics into their machine-readable travel documents (MRTDs), i.e. passports. Failure to do so meant a removal from the program. Unfortunately the public outcry on the invasion of privacy that biometrics on passports presents has been heard in many countries but has not halted the process. Hence many of us today that have visited the United States in the last five years have been forced to renew our passport into the MRTD format. US border controls involve formalities such as the use of a camera for facial recognition and fingerprinting.

There are some serious privacy concerns here above and beyond the obvious. Not only does this involve a central data store of fingerprints and photos (and face scans) that can be scanned against other databases for other purposes, but this sensitive information may be transferred to other countries when verification is required at border controls.

Living in the fast lane

A new growing trend for those travellers looking to skip the painstakingly slow border controls is a biometric ID that tells security screeners that a passenger has passed a background check and is not on the government terrorist watch list. This gives a free pass to the front of the security-checkpoint line that every passenger must pass through.

At the time of writing there were 17 airports in the United States offering Registered Traveller programs with customers paying US$100 each for the privilege plus a US$28 Transport Security Administration (TSA) vetting fee (http://www.flyclear. com). By January 2008 about 90,000 travellers had been accepted into the program nationwide (Goll 2008). For their money travellers still have their bags scanned and the ID card is no guarantee against a random search, although this is all done in a more effective way using advanced explosives detectors and iris scans to verify members' identities while simultaneously checking their shoes for bombs. Once the scans are complete the traveller can pass through security without showing IDs or having to remove footwear.

A new system of automated electronic gates at Dubai airport has been devised that will not only speed up the registration of travellers through the airport but also act as a significant barrier for illegal entrants into the Emirate. The electronic gates utilise the concepts of smart card and fingerprint identification to automate the registration process. This ensures that each person can only enrol once in the system. In the first month of its operation, the e-gate recorded a tremendous success with more than 3,500 residents from over 45 nationalities applying for a smart card that contains identification information. By May 2007 there were 450,000 cards in circulation and the number of e-gates at Dubai airport was increased to 16 (AME Info 2007). Travellers can choose not to use the e-gate system, although the system is popular with residents who travel frequently as it provides quicker processing through immigration at the airport.

In early 2008 Swedish airline SAS launched a new biometric system extending the biometric security program on national flights from Stockholm and Gothenburg that will be rolled out to international flights in the near future. You register your fingerprint when handing in your baggage and again at the gate. In this way you are automatically matched to your checked baggage. This makes the check-in process easier and improves security. The new system eliminates the need to show photographic ID. Your fingerprint is the means of identification and, after completion of the trip, your fingerprint in automatically erased by the system. The use of fingerprint ID is optional. Those who prefer may still travel with an identity card or passport.

Tracking our children

During the past five years developments in information technology have created unprecedented opportunities for observing children and young people, for supervising and controlling their activities and for gathering and sharing information about their lives. We have already covered the growing use of databases to store and share children's personal information: what has not been covered yet is the increasing number of commercially available devices that are used to track children's movements and habits. These range from the routine use of CCTV in schools or webcams in nurseries to devices that purport to reveal the exact location of a child at any given moment. It is now possible for a child to be under near-constant scrutiny throughout each day.

Location tracking is a widely provided service in many countries such as Finland, the UK and the United States. In Japan it is becoming an increasing practice to tag children and a major uniform maker in the UK is considering adding tracking devices (a spy in the waistband or a bug in the blazer) to school uniforms after a survey (Meikle 2007) found many parents would be interested in knowing where their offspring were.

Every child fingerprinted

'Britain is the only country in Europe to use biometric technology extensively in schools. While Ireland has low usage, their data commissioner has issued strict guidance to minimise any possible claims for damages from a student in future.'

ARCH, 2007b

There has been some publicity concerning the use of biometrics on children in UK schools. Early experiments in the use of retinal scans were halted because the process was too slow, so currently the type of biometric normally used is a child's thumb or fingerprint. School formalities have been expanded from the taking of the register of all present children, that parents of today are familiar with, to the fingerprinting of children. Fingerprinting of children in UK schools is used for buying lunch, the use of the library and even to register them in class. The director of ARCH Terri Dowty made the following comment:

> 'having fingerprint technology in schools – allowing students to register, use the library and buy canteen food . . . [was] encouraging children to be casual about their biometric data.'
>
> TERRI DOWTY, director of ARCH

UK schools started fingerprinting children in around 2002. Quietly encouraged by central government, parents were not generally informed. By 2007 more than 5,000 schools had fingerprinted children, some as young as five, although schools have since been encouraged to request the consent of the parents before taking biometric data of children.

School systems store fingerprint templates, the lifelong key to a person's identity. Within 10 years these will be used to authenticate bank accounts and passports. The main issue is that schools that are not equipped with secure systems designed to handle sensitive data are doing just this today. This risk of 'identity theft' is significant. The difference between identity theft from a fingerprint and an ID that you may get from your bank is that an ID on a bank card can be changed and the old one deactivated; the same cannot be said about your children's fingerprints.

Biometric systems are used not only for administrative convenience, they can also monitor children's behaviour because behind most biometric systems could be a database that can be mined. For example library systems can create reports of children's reading habits broken down by gender, age and ethnicity. Canteen systems monitor children's individual eating habits and can provide parents with printouts of their child's daily meal choices. Schools are encouraged to invest in biometric technologies and can even receive subsidies for this.

That is not all: children's private data is becoming ever more available to a wide range of people, but there is little awareness of the way in which this can be exploited commercially or the personal profiling that it allows. The fact is that any information that is digitised and linked to an identity has the potential to be profiled.

Mobile phones and GPS

The market in devices to track the physical location of children has been expanding steadily over the past few years. Typically equipment is promoted as offering parents the 'peace of mind' of knowing exactly where their children are, although in reality a device can only tell you its own location and not whether it is in the same place as the child being tracked.

Did you know that it is in fact quite easy to initiate tracking on a mobile phone without consent of the phone owner, as long as you have access to their phone when the SMS that says 'you are being tracked' arrives so you can delete it without the knowledge of the phone owner.

Until quite recently tracking has been carried out via children's mobile phones by calculating the relative signal strengths at three different mobile communications masts and 'triangulating' the phone's location from these.

Mobile phone location tracking receives information from the network about which cell your phone is currently in and for a small fee displays the location on an online map. In order to activate this service you need first to prove your identity, via a credit card, and then obtain consent from the owner of the phone in question to be tracked. Approval of tracking is done by sending an SMS message to the phone to which they must reply. It is in fact quite easy to initiate tracking on a mobile phone without the consent of the phone owner, as long as you have access to their phone when the SMS arrives.

The signal received from the device being tracked is superimposed onto a map that parents can view on a webpage or regular updates can be sent to their own mobile phones. Additional features allow parents to set boundaries or prescribe routes and receive an alert if the device leaves the pre-set area.

The potential for misuse or corrupt disclosure of child location information presents a significant threat to children's safety, particularly in circumstances where it is important that a family's home address is not known or where information is given to a person who may commit offences against a child.

On top of this is the fact that the constant surveillance of children is effectively treating children as passive objects of adult scrutiny. So what does that mean to us? Well we might be better wondering what 'having privacy' will mean to our children in 20 years time. We could then speculate on what the impact will be on the children that are not yet born.

Turning the offline world online with RFID

RFID is a technology that promises a world where virtually every item of goods we possess, from a packet of coffee to a car licence plate, will be communicating with transmitters–receivers embedded everywhere, from doorways to roadways to point-of-sale terminals effectively turning the offline world online. Everything we do offline or online can and will be tracked.

Some governments are using RFID in passports: Belgium was the first European country to do this. The privacy implications include the reading of RFID chips from rogue scanners. Early implementations of RFID in passports were not encrypted, but they are today to mitigate this risk.

By March 2006 over 1,800 RFID-related patents had been issued by the US Patent Office (Grimaila 2006). Just like satellite tracking devices, these chips will make it possible for governments around the world to mark individuals for surveillance purposes. RFID tags are being used today on criminals (minor offenders) effectively placing them in prison but free to continue working in their day-to-day lives. Scanners are placed at the offender's home enforcing a type of 'house arrest'. All movements are recorded by prison authorities. For example

167

if the offender is not registered as being home by 17:00 every day, they will face having their sentence lengthened or perhaps being sent to a traditional prison.

The idea of embedding RFID tags in clothes is also gaining momentum. In the UK, schools ran a pilot on selected pupils for the embedding of RFID tags in school uniforms in 2007. The pilot was a success and parents are in agreement with the schools who want to go the next step of embedding RFID tags in the entire school uniform. Key drivers for the schools are eliminating truancy and for parents a reduction in the risk that a child's school blazer will be lost or stolen.

> **Did you know that** RFID tags are small wireless devices that provide unique identifiers which can be read by remote sensors? RFID tags can be 'active' which means that they emit signals that can be sensed remotely. RFID tags are discrete hence it is not obvious that you have something that has a tag that may be transmitting information nor is it obvious that there is a reader in the proximity that is picking up the data.

In Sweden mine workers carry RFID chips on their uniforms. In the event of an accident, the chip will radio the miner's location to rescue crews. In Japan employers use the chips to monitor employee efficiency. Istanbul recently approved an RFID contract to install chips on its municipal vehicles.

The EU's Article 29 Data Protection Working Party examined the issue of RFID tags in the workplace in a working paper published in January 2005 (European Union 2005). The group recommended the increased visibility to employees and others of the RFID chip, the increased security of personal data, as well as the right of employees to correct stored data.

If RFID chips were embedded in your clothes it would mean that even if your personal information were not available, the store could identify from what you wear certain information about you when you walk in, e.g. are you wearing designer clothes? They would have scanners around the store that will sense your chips. A RFID tag in this situation might hold as much if not more value than the designer brand itself. For example it could be that you have a RFID tag that replaces the loyalty card from your favourite supermarket that profiles you as a vegetarian. Your supermarket and your favourite coffee shop are friends, i.e. they share information collected on you. Thus when you pass the coffee shop you receive a personalised advertisement that offers your favourite vegetarian snack, just for you. Another example is a nightclub in Barcelona offering VIP status which gives queue jumping privileges and free drinks to those customers willing to have an RFID chip implanted under the skin in their upper arm.

In fact the nightclub in Barcelona is a real example. Clubbers have had an RFID tag embedded under the skin and are enthusiastic about the freedom offered them; they do not need to carry cash as it is loaded on the chip. This is at least how it feels to the punters. In reality the chip holds a unique identifier that when scanned authorises the wearer to spend money that they have placed on account with the chip issuer. Other nightclubs that are looking to do the same just need to transfer each VIP customers' unique ID number to their databases already using the technology, hence one RFID implant will work for all customers to all nightclubs.

> RFID tags are so discrete that it is possible to embed them under the skin, and this is happening today both in animals, and in humans. There are some ethical questions concerning their use in humans. However the use of RFID has some very positive applications, e.g. in the United States whereby RFID has been used to help carers keep track of family members that suffer from Alzheimer's disease

Recall the section on the sharing of sensitive information. Hospital authorities are linking databases in order to provide a more available service. Let us develop this further with RFID. The general acceptance of such devices is driven by a growing desire for safety in our lives. Imagine if you are brought into an emergency room unconscious: a scanner in the hospital doorway could read the chip ID of your implanted RFID. Your medical records will be released from a database: your diabetes, penicillin allergy etc. Some US hospitals are already offering this service. Early adopters are those suffering from epilepsy, diabetics, Alzheimer's disease and other life-threatening illnesses that have an impact on how a patient should be treated. It replaces the traditional bracelet or necklace normally worn holding this type of information in paper format. The vision for the future is that this service should be available in all hospitals, so wherever the patient turns up they will be scanned and treated accordingly.

The only information kept on the chip is the patient ID which links to their medical records. This necessitates all hospitals to connect their databases. What this means is that it does not matter where the patient turns up, the scanned ID will be presented to the treating (and authorised) doctor independent of where the data was originally collected and stored. It is not too farfetched to speculate that a natural progression is the extension of this type of service to ambulance services.

This presents some questions that we may ask ourselves on what will happen next:

- Imagine the possibility that if your child was missing the implanted chip could be used to locate your child quickly and bring them back home. Would you agree to your children receiving RFID implants in the name of safety even knowing that everything about their activities was being logged? Will we start 'chipping' our children as social acceptance of the use of RFID implants spreads? Some parents do this today, and this service is being sold in the United States.
- What happens when RFID becomes linked to the GPS network? This is not as farfetched as it sounds. The main provider of school uniforms today in the UK (Truex) is looking at implanting chips into school uniforms and linking them to GPS.

The arguments for RFID implants could become somewhat persuasive, just as the use of biometrics in passports has gained momentum and increased public acceptance since 9/11. However there is still significant public resistance given their speculated risks to our personal privacy, particularly when we talk about embedding chips in humans in the same as we do in our cats and dogs today.

So what are the immediate risks? The chip itself holds a personal ID that is linked to your personal data if we take health records as an example. So there is a risk of 'rogue' scanners that can scan you as you walk by and pull out this number, but what are they going to do with it? Nothing unless they: (1) have authorisation to access the area of the hospital systems where your ID linked to your personal data is stored; (2) can hack in to the system; or (3) can impersonate you in a form of identity theft.

What about replacing loyalty cards with RFID? The risks here are basically the same as those that exist today; stores, airlines and hotel chains all share our personal data as quickly as it is collected, as we as the customers do not bother to tick the 'opt-out' box when given the chance. The only difference is that you will no longer need to present a card; you just walk into the store, hotel or receive your priority check-in service at the airline. You will be uniquely identified as a customer to one or more of the services and also what type of customer you are. Your details will automatically present themselves to whichever personnel happen to be assigned at your service. Your profile or customer type will in most cases influence how you will be treated.

In fact the biggest risk to our privacy is the linking of the databases, which is the strength behind the compelling arguments for RFID. This means that if you are chipped wherever you go your activities can be logged and stored. Your ID is unique and links to all data collected on you. So the greatest risk with RFID is not the chip itself. It is the fact that it uniquely identifies you, has become a part of you and links you directly to data stored and collected on you wherever this may be.

1. This is fine as long as you trust whoever is holding this information on you, based on what you know about

the holding authority today and what they may become tomorrow.

2. Identity theft will be more complete as the chip could link to everything that you are and what you do, although, unlike with biometrics, on discovery of identity theft stopping the fraud is just a matter of deactivating the chip: you could get a new RFID chip implant with a unique ID that will be linked to all of your personal data.

BIG BROTHER AWARDS GO TO PRIVACY INVADERS

Each year the national members and affiliated organisations of Privacy International present the 'Big Brother Awards' (Privacy International 2007) to the government and private sector organisations which have done the most to threaten personal privacy in their countries. Since 1998 over 40 ceremonies have been held in 16 countries, and hundreds of awards have given to some of the most powerful government agencies, individuals and corporations in those countries.

A 'Lifetime Menace' award is also presented. The juries worldwide consist of lawyers, academics, consultants, journalists and civil right activists that grant the award to the most deserving government institution or organisation in their country. Some examples of awards granted and the justification are given in this section.

Privacy International announces global privacy invaders

In an event in Montreal, Canada, Privacy International ran the International Big Brother Awards ceremony. There were winners from all over the world.

- **Most invasive company** was Choicepoint, for their vast databases of personal data, sold to nearly anyone who wishes to pay. Read the section on data aggregation companies for more information on Choicepoint.

- **Worst public official** was Stewart Baker, former general counsel for the National Security Agency and now undersecretary for policy at the Department of Homeland Security, behind and at the forefront of the most disastrous US surveillance policies, most recently the EU–US agreement on passenger name records transfers.

- **Most heinous government** was the UK government for being the greatest surveillance society amongst democratic nations, rivalling only Malaysia, China and Russia as it also leads other countries across the EU down the same path. More on this was given in the section on surveillance.

- **Most appalling project or technology** was won by the ICAO, a UN agency, for implementing a variety of invasive policies behind closed doors, including the 'biometric passport' and passenger data transfer deals. There is more information on the impact this has had on privacy not just in the United States but globally in the sections on the *USA Patriot Act* and on border controls.

- **Lifetime menace award** went to 'communitarianism' and the proponents of the 'common good' because every bad policy around the world is justified based on the philosophy that is good for society and the individual must sacrifice their selfish rights in favour of the needs of the many.

The Big Brother Awards are not just awarded globally but also by privacy organisations in each country. Some examples of awards presented in Australia and France are given in the following sections.

The Orwells in Australia

In 2006 the NSW Department of Health and the Swift financial transaction network both received Big Brother Awards. The Big Brother Awards in Australia are called 'The Orwells'.

'The failure to allow partitioning of sensitive health information, the lack of controls on authorized users, and failure to pilot both opt-in as well as opt-out systems could threaten public trust in what could be an immensely valuable tool for improving both individual and population health.'

DR ROGER MAGNUSSON,
judge at the 2006 Big Brother Awards

The Swift network (Society for Worldwide Interbank Financial Telecommunication) processes international fund transfers in Australia for the Commonwealth Bank, Wetspac and ANZ. Swift won the award for being the Greatest Corporate Invader of Privacy, with the NSW Department of Health winning the award for Most Invasive Technology for the electronic health record system.

The French Big Brother Awards

The French were busy in 2006: there were lots of winners. Nicolas Sarkozy the then French Minister of the Interior and today's President of France is the only person to have been nominated six times to the Big Brother Awards in France, although he did manage to get himself disqualified on the first occasion and then again on the seventh occasion in 2007, although this may have something to do with the fact that he was now President.

Some (and not all) of the 2006 Orwell prize winners for France are as follows.

- *Orwell Etat et élus* is the award given to the most intrusive member of the administration, public servant or member of parliament and it was Jacques Lebrot, 'security' vice prefect of Seine-St-Denis, who won by depriving employment to a few thousand workers after trusting a police census, violating their presumption of innocence on the basis of clearly discriminating practices (most workers were of Islamic faith).

- ***Orwell Entreprises*** is the award given to the most intrusive firm and Sony-BMG won this quite simply by incorporating a 'rootkit', a small spy program, in its commercialised audio CDs to monitor use by a purchaser. Once the CD is used on a computer the 'rootkit' has the capacity to bypass any security system and hence is able to gather information. As a result the spy program will leave a flaw in the customer's computer security system.

- ***Orwell Localités*** is the award given to the most intrusive city officials. It was won by Paul Anselin the Mayor of Ploërmel in the Morbihan, Brittany and the Conseil Général de Haute-Savoie, who jointly received the award for their enthusiastic eagerness to implement video surveillance. The Conseil Général de Haute-Savoie did particularly well in that he installed video surveillance systems in 10 of the 48 regional colleges but omitted to obtain authorisation from the CNIL (National Commission for Data Processing and Liberties) and forgot to notify parents and teachers.

- ***Orwell Novlang*** is the Newspeak Award and was given to Frédéric Péchenard head of the Paris Judiciary Police who encouraged the genetic filing of the local population under the pretence that 'the innocents could be cleared of all suspicion'.

- ***Orwell Ensemble de son Oeuvre*** is the Lifetime Menace Award which was handed to Pascal Clément 'garde des Sceaux' (Minister of Justice) who was nominated for imposing retroactively the wearing of electronic bracelets on sexual offenders after their release and in spite of the Constitution.

DO NOT GET HIGHJACKED

In this book we have discussed how we willingly share our personal information in the online information society and how our personal information can be collected and stored by government authorities and those organisations interested in making money from us. The Identity Linkage Matrix (Figure 5.4) gives examples of information that is collected about us and information that we share. This is mapped into the matrix depending on linkage to identity (i.e. physical persona) and how the personal information is organised. The mapping of information that is gathered on us or that we share can show us in a simple way the potential impact on our lives. The Identity Linkage Matrix has two axes and four quadrants: the higher the information is in the quadrant, the stronger the link to our identity; the further to the right of the quadrant, the easier it is for our personal information to be mined.

The horizontal axis represents information gathered or shared with how well structured this information is, and it is the vertical axis that represents whether there is some linkage of information gathered or shared to the real identity.

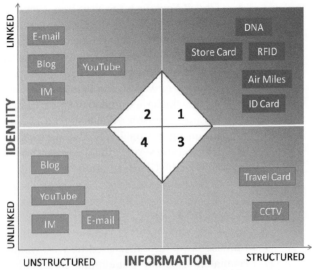

FIGURE 5.4   *The Identity Linkage Matrix (Öqvist 2007b)*

Information shared or gathered and placed in the top two quadrants is linked to our identity and has the potential to be mined with our identities, whereas information shared or gathered and placed in the bottom two quadrants is not linked, but there is potential of linkage via a 'dormant identity linkage', i.e. contamination of unlinked information or access to another information source that is linked.

Information linked directly to our identity and gathered using structured methods is placed in the 'hot' quadrant; the top right-hand corner. This data is: (a) most valuable to other people and (b) most damaging if used inappropriately. This quadrant is also the most interesting quadrant for those that want to profile us, e.g. government authorities, stores, airlines etc. and those with intentions to commit identity theft.

Some examples of the impacts of the Identity Linkage Matrix are given in Table 5.1. The numbers in the first column correspond to the numbers of the quadrants in Figure 5.4.

Let us take some examples from the matrix and see what this means.

CCTV is positioned in the matrix as information that is gathered in a structured way although it is not linked to our identity. This dislocation from our identity is dependent on the fact that the same person that has access to the information collected by CCTV does not also have access to digital data that is linked directly to your identity, i.e. a store card or RFID. If this was the case then your movements on camera are linked directly to your identity (dormant identity linkage). A good example is the surveillance cameras in the London Underground. If you use a travel card (such as an Oyster Card, a form of electronic ticketing used on Transport for London and some National Rail services within the Greater London area) that you have chosen to link to your identity (you can chose to use Oyster anonymously today), it makes the jobs of the police easier: they can see exactly the time that you swiped your card on the camera that is positioned to film you in the act.

RFID is in the "hot quandrant". The use of RFID in surveillance and tracking has the potential for growing acceptance

TABLE 5.1 *Identity Linkage Matrix impact examples (Öqvist 2007b)*

	Type of information gathered or shared	Identity linkage	Consequences	Existing examples
1	Structured	Yes	Intelligent data-mining is possible by authorised personnel. Profiles are attached to identity. Potential consequences today and in the future include influencing decisions that you make or choices being made for you. Risk of personal information exposure when information holder has insufficient security measures in place.	Government authorities, store cards, frequent flyer programs, congestion control (RFID linked to car number-plate that is in turn registered to your name).
2	Unstructured	Yes	Can be mined by interested parties, e.g. recruitment agencies. Information exposure, identity theft, online grooming of children, online bullying or harassment.	Blogging and social or professional networking spaces, forum activities etc. using real name.
3	Structured	No	Limited. Potential 'dormant identity linkage', e.g. police have authority to mine CCTV and other tracking technologies to link an identity.	CCTV, travel card paid by cash etc.

(Continued)

Table 5.1   *(Continued)*

	Type of information gathered or shared	Identity linkage	Consequences	Existing examples
4	Unstructured	No	Limited. Potential 'dormant identity linkage', thus same risks as when linked.	Blogging and social or professional networking spaces, forum activities etc. using an alias

as has been demonstrated in the use of cameras for surveillance in the UK and the United States. Likewise, the decision to permit RFID to be included in school uniforms in the UK has been approved. This enables children's movements to be tracked wherever there are sensors. A related vision for the future in the UK is the linking of national databases holding residents personal information into one or more master repositories, which can be mined and leveraged to improve government services and fight crime more effectively (The Royal Academy of Engineering 2007). In the UK and the United States there are plans to merge hospital databases on a national level. Hence everything we do in our everyday lives will have the potential to not only be tracked, but also to be mined. The more personal or sensitive the information is that is accessible by the use of a unique ID linked directly to our identity, the more interesting a target it will be for tomorrow's hackers and those involved in the growing trend of cyber-warfare. Information that can be effectively mined can be used to influence choices and decisions we make in our lives both knowingly and unknowingly, today and tomorrow.

Social networking spaces are where we share our personal information in blogs and online networking communities in an unstructured format. We cannot be sure of what happens to information once it has been shared online and if we change our mind about any published material it is too late. It has most likely been copied and replicated to another server or indexed and cached by some search engine. This information has the potential to be mined, even though it is unstructured, by interested parties. Stories of paedophiles profiling their victims are some of the most publicised examples.

6 Our Choice of Future

We all live in an environment that comprises controllable and uncontrollable factors and the grey areas between. In those grey areas we theoretically have the power to influence decisions made about how our personal data is being managed on a national level in democratic societies. However the use of surveillance has grown and public resistance is marginal due to the overriding motivation for a safe society and a growing desire for an easy life. The use of surveillance and tracking technologies has the potential for growing acceptance, as has the linking of all national databases holding residents personal information into one or more master repositories, which that can be mined and leveraged to improve government services and fight crime more effectively. The message is clear: the 'information age' has unleashed a surveillance society that feeds on our imaginary fear fuelled by media hype. We are on the cusp of a new surveillance era.

For this reason you will not be aware of when and where you are being surveyed or tracked. The technology is here with microscopic surveillance: tracking technologies and sensors that turn the offline world online. Everything tracked will be stored in a database. In this world you will have no choice about whether and when you are being surveyed or tracked. Furthermore your children will not think to question its logic, because they have grown up accustomed to the notion of 'being tracked' as the norm. In fact the current generation could be the last generation to question the rational.

So what comes next? Well you can speculate: today you can see the cameras, i.e. you know that you are being watched; tomorrow the cameras will be so small that the all pervasive surveillance will be invisible to you, and to all of us. You will not be aware that you are being watched. You will just feel safe because you know that they are out there, always watching.

What will be the long-term consequences if you continue to permit yourself to be tracked in the offline and online world, without enforcing your right to know what is being tracked and how your personal information is being used? Does it not concern you, that personal or sensitive information that has been collected and stored in the past has the potential to be damaging to what you want to achieve today, tomorrow or sometime in the future? Even if you are uneasy, is it in any case too late to do anything now? After all it is like a roller-coaster on tracks that seem to go nowhere, a carriage that is driven by the force of its own momentum, and equipped with brakes that do not work.

So what if it is too late, could the vision of a transparent society offer a compromise for a future destination? If not, what are you going to do to slow or reverse the trend towards this more open way of being? Perhaps you will proceed to change how you normally share your personal information? Or what about adding your voice to the millions which are united in a utopian dream of keeping privacy in a way that we understand today?

Nevertheless you live in an information society whereby you have joined the ranks of information junkies with an inability to 'turn-off': the 'always on' syndrome, a malady of an age that risks making your short time in this world meaningless, reduced to the level of being a slave to SMS messages, the telephone, blogging, and email. There is a continual barrage that swamps your mind until you forget about those basic things in life which you used to do, that made you feel good about being human and alive.

From another perspective you are a part of an information society that has given you a voice. The voices of many individuals are giving power to the people in a way never experienced before. Online you are equal, you are not judged by what colour you are, which religion you follow, by how much you weigh or on your ability to communicate. This is equality in the beautiful sense of the word. We all matter, although in the same breath, given the number of us online having that conversation, you may feel insignificant. You may feel that as a part of the whole, each one of us individually equates to nothing, like a needle in the haystack, a particle of dust flouting around in the air we breathe, a grain of sand on the beach, or an atom in our universe that will exist just briefly in the infinite space of time. Thus is it not bizarre that it is in fact quite the opposite that has occurred? We are all part of the same conversation and it grows because of this: the conversation has become an extension of our physical selves.

As your conversation evolves it sprouts legs, becomes mobile and strong and has the power to influence thinking in the world. The conversation enables you to feel part of a community, a community that matters to you, where you have a voice and where you can be sure that someone out there is listening and interested in hearing what you have to say.

Notes

1. 'Virtual Visitation' has many names: Virtual Parent-Time, Internet Visitation, Computer Visitation and others. The common legal term is 'Virtual Visitation' and that is what we will refer to it as, although it may vary from state to state or individual preference. 'Virtual Visitation' involves using tools such as personal video conferencing, Video Call, Video Chat, Email, Instant Messaging (IM), Video Email, camera phones, video phones and other wired or wireless technologies over the internet or other communication media. It is to supplement *not* replace in-person visits and telephone contact between a non-custodial parent and their children and the custodial parent when the children are with the non-custodial parent.

2. Curling is a team sport with similarities to bowls and shuffle board, played by two teams of four players each on a rectangular sheet of carefully prepared ice.

3. A 'slam book' is a notebook which is passed among school students normally when sitting in class. The keeper of the book starts by posing a question (which in the context of this section on bullying, 'Who is the most stupid boy in this class'?) and the book is then passed round for each of the other students to fill in their own answer to the question.

4. Fipr, an independent body that studies the interaction between information technology and society: its goal is to identify technical developments with significant social impact, commission and undertake research into public policy alternatives, and promote public understanding and dialogue between technologists and policymakers in the UK and Europe.

5. To demonstrate due diligence means that you need to have the security mechanisms in place to minimise the chance of damage or exposure, accidental or malicious, to insured assets, e.g. installing a fire alarm demonstrates due diligence so if a fire occurs the consequential damage should be reduced.

6. The Swedish personal ID number is represented as the date of birth of the holder with an extra four digits, even numbers for females and odd numbers for males, in the format 'YYMMDD-xxxx'.

References and Further Reading

About.com (2008a) The history of the electric telegraph and telegraphy. http://inventors.about.com/od/tstartinventions/a/telegraph.htm (accessed 21 September 2008).

About.com (2008b) The history of the telephone—Alexander Graham Bell. http://inventors.about.com/od/bstartinventors/a/telephone.htm (accessed 21 September 2008).

Alsanea, R. (2008) *Girls of Riyadh*. Penguin Books Ltd.

AME Info (2007) More e-gates at Dubai airport. AME Info, 22 May. http://www.ameinfo.com/121024.html (accessed 21 September 2008).

Anderson, R. et al. (2006) Children's databases—safety and privacy. Foundation for Information Policy Research. http://www.cl.cam.ac.uk/%7Erja14/Papers/kids.pdf (accessed 21 September 2008).

APEC (2005) What is the APEC Privacy Framework? http://www.apec.org/apec/news_media/fact_sheets/apec_privacy_framework.html (accessed 21 September 2008).

ARCH (2007a) Select Committee on Merits of Statutory Instruments—Twenty-Seventh Report. http://www.publications.parliament.uk/pa/ld200607/ldselect/ldmerit/146/14608.htm (accessed 21 September 2008).

ARCH (2007b) Child Tracking: Biometrics in Schools and Mobile Location Devices. http://www.arch-ed.org/issues/Tracking%20devices/final_report_on_child_tracking.htm.

BBC News (2004) Watchdog's Big Brother UK warning. BBC News, 16 August. http://news.bbc.co.uk/2/hi/uk_news/politics/3568468.stm (accessed 20 September 2008).

Beck, C. (2007) Getting past the conversation bottleneck. *The Age of Conversation.* http://www.ageofconversation.com (accessed 21 September 2008).

Boyd, D. (1998) http://www.danah.org/papers/KnowledgeTree. pdf (accessed 20 September 2008).

Boyd, D. (2007a) Social network sites: public, private, or what? The Knowledge Tree, 13 May. http://kt.flexiblelearning.net.au/ tkt2007/edition-13/social-network-sites-public-private-or-what/ (accessed 20 September 2008).

Boyd, D. (2007b) Why youth (heart) social network sites: the role of networked publics in teenage social life. http://www.danah. org/papers/WhyYouthHeart.pdf (accessed 20 September 2008).

Boyd, D. and Heer, J. (2006) Profiles as conversation: networked identity performance on Friendster. http://www.danah.org/ papers/HICSS2006.pdf (accessed 20 September 2008).

Brin, D. (1998) *The Transparent Society.* Perseus Books, Jackson, TN.

Brown, D. (2001) J.D.1, Developing strategies for collecting and presenting grooming evidence in a high tech world. http://www.ndaa.org/publications/newsletters/update_ volume_14_number_11_2001.html.

CBC News (2007) Student recruits unfit for service, say former border guards. CBCnews.ca, 1 October. http:// www.cbc.ca/canada/british-columbia/story/2007/10/01/bc-borderguards.html (accessed 20 September 2008).

CHALLENGE (2006) The Treaty of Prüm and the Principle of Loyalty. CHALLENGE Liberty & Security, 4 December. http://www.libertysecurity.org/article1186.html (accessed 21 September 2008).

Chandler, C. (2006) The Great Firewall of China. *Fortune,* 6 March. http://money.cnn.com/magazines/fortune/fortune_ archive/2006/03/20/8371819/index.htm (accessed 26 November 2008).

Council of Europe (1950) *Convention for the Protection of Human Rights and Fundamental Freedoms.* http://conventions. coe.int/Treaty/en/Summaries/Html/005.htm (accessed 13 October 2008).

Delta Sky Magazine (2006) http://www.internetvisitation. org/pdf/Delta-Sky%20Magazine%20Sept%202006.pdf (September).

Elon University (2008) Imagining the internet. Predictions database. Pew Internet & American Life Project. http:// www.elon.edu/predictions/internethistory.aspx (accessed 21 September 2008).

European Commission (1995) *EU Directive on Data Privacy (95/46/EC).* http://ec.europa.eu/justice_home/fsj/privacy/ law/index_en.htm (accessed 21 September 2008).

European Union (2005) Article 29 Data Protection Working Party 10107/05/EN WP105, 19 January. http://ec.europa.eu/ justice_home/fsj/privacy/docs/wpdocs/2005/wp105_en.pdf (accessed 21 September 2008).

Export Gov (2008) *Helping U.S. Companies Export, Welcome to the Safe Harbor.* http://www.export.gov/safeHarbor/.

Federal Trade Commission (1998) *Children's Online Privacy Protection Act of 1998.* http://www.ftc.gov/ogc/coppa1.htm (accessed 21 September 2008).

Ferraro, M. M. and Casey, E. (2005) *Investigating Child Exploitation and Pornography: The Internet, The Law and Forensic Science.* Academic Press.

Fipr (2008) Open letter to the Information Commissioner, 17 March. http://www.fipr.org/080317icoletter.html (accessed 21 September 2008).

Flood, M. (2003) *Regulating Youth Access to Pornography.* Centre for Women's Studies, Australian National University, http://www.usq.edu.au/course/material/CMS3011/Other/ TeenPornReport.pdf.

Goll, D. (2008) Some Oakland airport passengers will have a Clear advantage. *East Bay Business Times*, 28 January. http://www.bizjournals.com/eastbay/stories/2008/01/28/story14.html?page=2 (accessed 13 October 2008).

Gorski, K. (2007) WRITE. *The Age of Conversation*. http://www.ageofconversation.com (accessed 21 September 2008).

Graham, S. (2002) CCTV: the stealthy emergence of a fifth utility? http://www.casa.ucl.ac.uk/cyberspace/stephen_graham_fifth_utility.pdf (accessed 21 September 2008).

Hitwise (2008a) Facebook sees 40 percent growth year over year. Hitwise, 23 July. http://www.hitwise.com/press-center/hitwiseHS2004/us-facebook-grows-40-percent-23072008.php (accessed 21 September 2008).

Hitwise (2008b) Hitwise UK social networking update. Hitwise, 22 July. http://www.hitwise.co.uk/press-center/hitwiseHS2004/uk-facebook-22072208.php (accessed 21 September 2008).

HMSO (2004) *The Children's Act*. http://www.opsi.gov.uk/acts/acts2004/ukpga_20040031_en_1 (accessed 13 October 2008).

Impact Lab (2003) Information addiction. Impact Lab, 6 July. http://www.impactlab.com/2003/07/06/information-addiction/ (accessed 21 September 2008).

Information Commissioner's Office (1998) *The Data Protection Act*. http://www.ico.gov.uk/what_we_cover/data_protection.aspx (accessed 21 September 2008).

Madden, M., Fox, S., Smith, A. and Vitak, J. (2007) Digital footprints. Pew Internet & American Life Project. http://www.pewinternet.org/PPF/r/229/report_display.asp (accessed 13 October 2008).

Marlow, C., Naaman, M., Boyd, D. and Davis, M. (2006) HT06, Tagging Paper, Taxonomy, Flickr, Academic Article, ToRead. http://www.danah.org/papers/Hypertext2006.pdf (accessed 20 September 2008).

McLellan, G. H. (2007) The age of conversation. http://www.ageofconversation.com (accessed 20 September 2008).

Meikle, J. (2007) Pupils face tracking bugs in school blazers. *The Guardian*, 21 August. http://www.guardian.co.uk/uk/2007/aug/21/schools.education (accessed 13 October 2008).

Microsoft (2008) Microsoft HealthVault. http://www.healthvault.com/ (accessed 20 September 2008).

NationMaster.com (2008a) Development of the printing press. http://www.nationmaster.com/encyclopedia/Moveable-type (accessed 21 September 2008).

NationMaster.com (2008b) Video game addiction. http://www.nationmaster.com/encyclopedia/Video-game-addiction (accessed 21 September 2008).

NationMaster.com (2008c) Lee Seung Seop. http://www.nationmaster.com/encyclopedia/Lee-Seung-Seop (accessed 21 September 2008).

New Scientist (2007) Internet levels playing field for people with autism. *New Scientist*, 2 July. http://alameda.networkofcare.org/mh/news/detail.cfm?articleID=15170 (accessed 21 September 2008).

O'Connell, R. (2003) A typology of child cybersexploitation and online grooming practices. *The Guardian*, 24 July. http:// image.guardian.co.uk/sys-files/Society/documents/2003/ 07/24/Netpaedoreport.pdf (accessed 21 September 2008).

Öqvist, K. L. (2007a) Identity linkage and privacy. *ISSA J.*, April, 13–16.

Öqvist, K. L. (2007b) Identity linkage and privacy—Part 2. *ISSA J.*, December, 29–34.

ORNL (2008) Human Genome Project information. http://www.ornl.gov/sci/techresources/Human_Genome/home.shtml (accessed 21 September 2008).

Orwell, G. (1949) *Nineteen Eighty-Four*. Secker and Warburg: London.

OUT-LAW.com (2008) Lords overrule courts, criticise Scottish Information Commissioner. http://www.out-law.com/page-9247 (accessed 21 September 2008).

PKU-laboratoriet (2008) http://www.karolinska.se/templates/Page.aspx?id=44840&epslanguage=SV (accessed 21 September 2008).

Privacy International (2006a) Privacy and Human Rights 2006. http://www.privacyinternational.org/index.shtml?cmd[342][]=c-1-Privacy+and+Human+Rights&als[theme]=Privacy%20and%20Human%20Rights&conds[1][category........]=Privacy%20and%20Human%20Rights (accessed 13 October 2008).

Privacy International (2006b) Privacy Topics - Location Privacy 18/12/2007. http://www.privacyinternational.org/article.shtml?cmd[347]</a>=x-347-559093&als[theme]=Privacy%20and%20Human%20Rights (accessed 20 October 2008).

Privacy International (2007) Privacy International announces global privacy invaders. http://www.privacyinternational.org/article.shtml?cmd%5B347%5D=x-347-553112 (accessed 21 September 2008).

Privacy International (2008a) About Privacy International. http://www.privacyinternational.org/article.shtml?cmd[347]=x-347-65428 (accessed 21 September 2008).

Privacy International (2008b) Overview of privacy, aspects of privacy. http://www.privacyinternational.org/article.shtml?cmd[347]=x-347-55902 (accessed 21 September 2008).

Privacy International (2008c) Privacy International reports on Asia-Pacific privacy process. http://www.privacyinternational.org/article.shtml?cmd[347]=x-347-561712&als[theme]=Data%20Protection%20and%20Privacy%20Laws (accessed 21 September 2008).

Privacy International (2008d) DNA and genetic privacy. http://www.privacyinternational.org/index.shtml?cmd[342][]= c-1-DNA+and+Genetic+Privacy&als[theme]=DNA%20 and%20Genetic%20Privacy&conds[1][category.........]= DNA%20and%20Genetic%20Privacy (accessed 21 September 2008).

Privacy International (2008e) REAL ID Act passed by Congress. http://www.privacyinternational.org/article.shtml?cmd[347]= x-347-210373&als[theme]=National%20ID%20Cards (accessed 21 September 2008).

Raper Larenaudie, S. (2008) Riyadh Postcard. *Time*, 22 February. http://www.time.com/time/specials/2007/article/0,28804, 1714683_1714625_1714284,00.html (accessed 26 November 2008).

SFGate (2005) SFGate Home of the *San Francisco Chronicle*, 20 February. http://www.sfgate.com/cgi-bin/article.cgi?file=/c/ a/2005/02/20/MNGBKBEJO01.DTL (accessed 21 September 2008).

Stoll, C. (2000) *The Cuckoo's Egg: Tracking a Spy through the Maze of Computer Espionage.* Pocket.

Surveillance Studies Network (2006) *A Report on the Surveillance Society For the Information Commissioner,* Public Discussion Document, September 2006. http://www. ico.gov.uk/upload/documents/library/data_protection/ practical_application/surveillance_society_full_report_ 2006.pdf.

The Economist (2006a) Survey New Media: It's the links, stupid. *The Economist*, 20 April (print edn).

The Economist (2006b) Survey New Media: Compose yourself. *The Economist*, 20 April (print edn).

The Local (2005) Tsunami remembered in Sweden and Thailand. The Local Sweden's News in English, 26 December. http://www.thelocal.se/2749/20051226/ (accessed 21 September 2008).

The Royal Academy of Engineering (2007) *Dilemmas of Privacy and Surveillance—Challenges of Technological Change.* The Royal Academy of Engineering, London.

The Wall Street Journal Online (2007) Is this man cheating on his wife, 10 August, http://vhil.stanford.edu/news/2007/wsj-cheating.pdf.

Time Magazine (2006) The person of the year is you! *Time Magazine*, December 2006.

Time Magazine (2007) What Gen Y really wants. *Time Magazine*, 5 July. http://www.time.com/time/magazine/article/0,9171, 1640395,00.html (accessed 21 September 2008).

Tribune Wire (2008) Google Health. *The Tribune Wire*, 20 May. http://www.orlandosentinel.com/business/chi-google-health-080520-ht,0,6349009.story (accessed 20 September 2008).

United Nations (1948) *Universal Declaration of Human Rights 1948.* http://www.un.org/Overview/rights.html (accessed 13 October 2008).

United Nations (1966) *International Covenant on Civil and Political Rights.* http://www.hrcr.org/docs/Civil&Political/ intlcivpol.html (accessed 13 October 2008).

US Department of Health and Human Services (1996) *Health Insurance Portability and Accountability Act.* The United States Department of Health and Human Services, Office of Civil Rights. http://www.hhs.gov/ocr/hipaa/ (accessed 13 October 2008).

US Senate Committee on Banking, Housing, and Urban Affairs (1999) Information regarding the *Gramm–Leach–Bliley Act* of 1999. http://banking.senate.gov/conf/ (accessed 21 September 2008).

Weinburger, D. (2006) The wiki principle. *The Economist*, 20 April (print edn).

Index